Velvet Antlers, Velvet Noses

Velvet Antlers, Velvet Noses

The story of the only free-ranging
reindeer herd in Britain

Tilly Smith

Hodder & Stoughton

A CIP catalogue record for this title is available
from the British Library

ISBN 0-340-63825-7

Designed by Behram Kapadia
Typeset by Sally Kapadia
Printed and bound in Great Britain by Mackays of Chatham PLC

Hodder and Stoughton Ltd,
a division of Hodder Headline PLC
338 Euston Road
London NW1 3BH

To Alan, Alex and Fiona

Contents

Contents

Illustrations

Photographic credits

Introduction

I must be crazy, definitely off my head, to agree to write a book. My day is already full and chaotic. First there are the children to get to school. Then perhaps it is my turn to go up the hill and find the reindeer, ready for visitors at 11 a.m. What are we going to have for supper tonight? Should I replenish the fridge or can it last another day? Anything to postpone a trip to the shops. At least there is one good thing about leading a hectic life: it is a good excuse for putting off the housework. No one could describe me as house-proud.

The telephone rings. A shopping-centre wants to know what a Santa's Arrival by real reindeer involves. Switch into Christmas mode. Wonder while I talk whether they realise what a beautiful view I have from my office window. Just as I settle down to answer some letters the school bus rolls up and two starving children head into the house, throw down their jackets and rucksacks and, like a couple of fledglings, require filling with food.

While I scuttle from one task to another, from reindeer business to being a mother, Alan doggedly sticks to projects on the scale of the Forth Road Bridge: repairing or replacing miles of fencing out on the open hill; constructing new reindeer sheds, wooden walkways and outhouses; renovating a derelict farmhouse and keeping a check on the reindeer wherever they are on the hills.

One wishes there were a few more hours in the day. By bedtime I suspect we shall be wishing there were not so many. So I would like to say a special thank you to Judith Draper whose skill and patience were what turned the turmoil into a book.

CHAPTER ONE

Jingle Bells

I t was the week before Christmas and Santa Claus was due to pay a most important visit. The children from our local playgroup in Aviemore had thought of nothing else all morning. What would Santa bring them? Would he be the jolly old party on the Christmas cards, dressed in red with a long white beard? And, most important of all, would he really come by sleigh, with real live reindeer?

Excitement mounted at the village hall, where the children, their mothers and the play-leader had assembled. Suddenly a voice announced, "He's here!" and two dozen pairs of eager young eyes focused expectantly on the doors at the end of the hall. As they swung open there, framed in the doorway, was the round, smiling figure of Santa, resplendent in his regulation red suit and accompanied by the most beautiful reindeer, complete with huge antlers.

As Santa stepped forward to greet the children Larch, the reindeer, dutifully made to follow him. And that was when disaster struck. Negotiating antlers through doorways is, as you can imagine, a tricky business even for a reindeer and Larch, experienced though he was at this sort of thing, needed a little time to manoeuvre his way successfully into the hall.

Alas, the doorman, his mind evidently elsewhere, chose totally the wrong moment to let go of the heavy door. It swung back and with a resounding crack knocked one of Larch's antlers clean off his head. Experienced Christmas reindeer that he was, Larch carried on, lopsidedly, with his duties. If he was feeling foolish and embarrassed, he never let on. The look of horror on the faces of the play-leader and the mothers was worth going a long way to see. And I seem to remember that I had a rather un-Christmas-like word or two with the doorman.

Not all Christmas reindeer appearances get off to quite such a dramatic start, thank goodness, though loss of antlers (usually through natural causes) can present last-minute problems. Shopping-centre managers who have spent good money to have eye-catching reindeer parading with their Father Christmases hardly want antlerless ones, or a comical-looking pair with only one antler each – both on the same side.

What the average person does not realise is that Christmas comes perilously close to the time when male reindeer would normally cast their antlers in the wild, ready to grow a new set in the spring, and I have had many a heartache about a Christmas reindeer losing his at the worst possible moment. In fact, there have actually been occasions when we have had no option but to harness up two reindeer with only one antler each – one with the left side still intact, the other with the right – in a desperate attempt to make them look like a normal pair. Sometimes, I have to admit, I do not think the public even notice, though to be fair they have probably never seen a reindeer before anyway.

One person who could not have failed to see that one of his guests was somewhat "bald" on top was a shopping-centre manager in Birkenhead. As usual we were getting set up out of sight of the public in the loading bay area, ready for our appearance. The reindeer had been unloaded from the lorries, tethered and given a dish of food each. The manager had come down to admire them and we were passing the time of day with him, explaining the whys and wherefores of reindeer habits. As we stood chatting, Johan suddenly gave his head a rather more vigorous shake than normal. Alan and I watched in dismay as one of his antlers pinged off his head and, almost in slow motion, somersaulted to the ground. During the stunned silence which followed Johan was the only one who looked pleased.

"Does this normally happen?" asked the centre manager at last, somewhat tersely and obviously questioning the wisdom of spending money on such unpredictable creatures.

We played the incident down, explaining that reindeer do, of course, cast their antlers every year – it is just that some do it sooner than others and you can never be sure when it is going to happen. Since you cannot stick them back on, experience has taught us that it is best to take spare reindeer along whenever we make Christmas appearances, just in case.

The reindeer have been attending Christmas events for many years, long before we officially took over the herd in 1989. In the western world reindeer and Father Christmas have gone hand in hand for a long time, certainly since the early nineteenth century, when the American poet, Clement C. Moore, wrote a poem to his children entitled 'The Night Before Christmas'. In this he describes Father Christmas as an elf-like man, rosy cheeked and smoking a pipe. His sleigh is pulled by a team of eight reindeer – Dancer and Prancer, Donner and Blitzen, Comet and Cupid, Vixen and Dasher. Rudolph, the name that has (sadly in my opinion) become synonymous with reindeer, came later, from the song 'Rudolph the Red-Nosed Reindeer'. It was written in 1939 and took a swipe at America's alcohol prohibition laws.

From the day the ancestors of our reindeer first set hoof in Scotland, imported by a Swedish Lapp, Mikel Utsi, and his wife Dr Lindgren in 1952, there has been keen local interest in them. Very early on Mr Utsi established a tradition of training some of the castrated males and harnessing one of them up to his Lappish sleigh, which would then attend the children's Christmas party in Aviemore, to the great delight of the local people. It is a tradition that continues to this day. The difference is that nowadays the reindeer attending the local events on Christmas Day will have already had a busy schedule during November and December, delivering Father Christmas to shopping-centres all over the country, doing occasional modelling sessions for Christmas catalogues and, most rewarding, visiting hospitals and old people's homes.

On one occasion when we had agreed to visit a children's ward we found at the last minute that the only way to get there was by lift. Alan was concerned that the reindeer might be agitated, especially by the mirrors inside the lift, but they did not bat an eyelid. The only person with a problem was the porter who was deputed to scuttle along behind us with a bucket. Reindeer produce dry, rabbit-like droppings which tend to roll about on well-polished corridor floors. I had with me a lovely old reindeer called Keith, whom I took to see a girl with a broken leg. When Keith rested his head on her bed she was chuffed to bits.

We soon found that reindeer are amazingly good at travelling round the country. We load them in lorries big enough to take four racehorses. Unlike horses, though, they travel together in groups, not in separate stalls. They are social animals and like to be together though, because of their antlers, they need plenty of room. The sleigh goes in the lorry first then, when you have caught your reindeer, you simply lead them to the ramp, let go of the lead ropes and in they walk. We remove their halters and once they are out on the open road they lie down. We usually take four adults and two young ones and have found that they travel best if they are split into two groups, with two adults and one young one in each. I have often travelled in the back of the lorry with them and find that they always get out of each other's way, settling down in their own favourite spot each time.

Reindeer need to keep cool, so they must have plenty of ventilation when they are travelling. If we are on a long journey south (we have a base in Cambridge for the weeks leading up to Christmas), we stop on the way to feed and water them, though we tend not to take them out en route – if you suddenly start unloading reindeer beside the motorway you get rather a lot of people grinding to a halt to watch. Sometimes, though, I cannot resist telling people what we are carrying. I might go into a petrol station and, while paying for my fuel, see a poor cashier looking bored out of her mind.

"Have you ever seen a reindeer?" I say.

"No," she will answer, looking at me a trifle askance.

"Would you like to?"

"Y...e...s..." So I take her out into the car park and open the little side door and there will be a reindeer's head peering down at her. It can really make someone's day.

Almost without exception we find that people absolutely love reindeer and everybody wants to touch them. When they are tethered before or after an event they are not keen on being stroked and petted, but once they are in harness they seem to know that it is all part of the job and will tolerate any amount of touching. In fact, they take the whole business of Christmas parades all in their stride.

We usually plan to arrive at a centre a couple of hours beforehand so that we can unload the reindeer, give them a bowl of food and let them relax, tethered on a long rope. Then about half an hour before the event is due to start the sleighs are brought out, we get dressed up and the reindeer are harnessed up. The normal routine is to do a pre-planned circular route round the town, finishing up at the front of the shopping-centre. The route is advertised in advance and often there will be a local band to play a fanfare for the reindeer. The only problem is that most bands tend to march fairly fast and reindeer are slow walkers, so if you are not careful you end up miles behind.

You never quite know what to expect, either, as all events are different. When we arrived at one last year, the centre manager announced that there were a lot of animal protesters there, people who did not even think it right to use a horse for riding, and that someone from the RSPCA was turning up to watch. Of course we had nothing to hide, but it still made us a bit edgy. When the inspector turned up we showed him the lorry and he looked at the reindeer, then he said he was going to walk in the parade with us. Expecting to meet up with protesters, we were faced, instead, with a 10,000-strong crowd, all wanting to see reindeer. As we walked up the street there were still great waves of people coming in. The police were totally unable to control them. Yet the reindeer walked along totally unperturbed.

When we reached the end of the parade we could not get through the crowds to the bandstand where we were to pen the reindeer off and let them eat the lichen we had brought for them. It was only with great difficulty that we managed to unharness them from the sleigh.

"Would you mind holding this reindeer, please?" I asked the RSPCA inspector politely. A look of complete horror crossed his face, as Alan and I left him and set about clearing the way ahead. When we eventually led our team into the enclosure of the bandstand the inspector was astounded. He said that even police horses would not have tolerated the crush the reindeer had faced that day.

People imagine that it must take a long time to train

them but generally speaking they are quick to learn. The first thing is to teach them to lead on a halter, something we like to do when they are calves or yearlings, although older reindeer take to it quite well, too. The worst part is the initial stage of leading them away from the herd. It is particularly important to take more than one, so that they are company for each other. Once they are out of sight of the herd they begin to give up resisting and go with you more easily.

The main path off the hill is narrow and situated on the side of the hill, which makes even the most jumpy reindeer more inclined to follow behind you. By the time he has negotiated the bridge over the burn at the bottom and reached the road on the other side, the apprentice Christmas reindeer is virtually halter-trained. After that it is just a question of practice makes perfect.

It sounds easy and often is, though there are exceptions to the rule. There appear to be two types of reindeer: those who run ahead of you when you first put them on a halter and those who are stubborn and do not want to go with you at all. The ones who run ahead are easy to train: it means that they are willing and before long you can persuade them to walk behind you. The stubborn ones' first reaction is to lie down. They take a bit longer to train.

As a general rule reindeer like to be led on a long rein. They carry their heads very low when they are walking, so being on a long lead makes it easier for them to follow quietly. The mistake most people make is to hold the rope very close to the reindeer's face, which always makes them throw their heads about. Usually the only other animal people have experience of leading is a horse. But there is a big difference between a reindeer and a horse: those bony structures on top of their heads which can so easily get tangled up in a halter rope. It takes only a few fast twirls of the head for a stroppy reindeer to encase its antlers in rope – a further good reason for keeping the rope low down, away from the antlers.

One of the golden rules of leading reindeer is never let go. If you do, particularly on the hill, that can be the last you see of them for a while, as they leg it with rope trailing from the halter. Our children, Alex and Fiona, have had this rule instilled into them from the day they first wanted to lead their own reindeer. Unfortunately, the law of force dictates that something pulling an object lighter than itself will inevitably win, as Fiona found to her cost. She had asked to lead Crackle down off the hill, while I led a smaller bull, Emperor. Crackle was behaving fine, so I let her. All went well until we got to the carpark and prepared to put them in the back of the van. While I was getting the doors open something spooked Crackle and he bolted. Fiona hung on like a rag doll and was dragged from boulder to boulder up the path. Eventually, she could hang on no longer and was left lying in a heap on the ground. I ran up with Emperor to find her sitting up in floods of tears. But she was fine. "Look after Fiona, Alex," I said and headed up after Crackle with Emperor to retrieve the situation.

Handling the reindeer from when they are calves, bringing them down off the hill to the house in the back of the van, and then taking a couple of them with the older males to do the Christmas circuit gets them so accustomed to travelling and to the strange sights and sounds that, when they become adults and their turn comes to pull a sleigh, they take it all in their stride.

Because people naturally want reindeer with antlers at Christmas we only use gelded males, who tend to keep theirs that bit longer than the breeding bulls. We do not geld them until they are three. As the Sami people (the Lapps) discovered, if you geld reindeer too young it stunts their growth. The females, or cows, are not suitable because they are not as big and impressive looking as the geldings and anyway most will be in calf in the run-up to Christmas, which rules out sleigh-pulling.

Training a reindeer to go in harness can take as little as a day or as long as a week, depending on the individual concerned. The most difficult one I can recall was Parsley, who had spent part of his life at Whipsnade. Because he had been in a zoo for two years and had not been handled he was terribly nervous and it took us a whole summer to get him to settle. We used to take him for walks round the forest on a lead rope to give him confidence. He eventually became a very good sleigh-pulling reindeer.

Reindeer training starts at the beginning of October. It cannot be done in the summer because their antlers are still in velvet and are easily damaged, and also it is too hot for them to work. The young ones are always trained alongside older ones who have already done it lots of times. First they are fitted with the wooden collars which hang round their necks and a broad belt with bells on top goes under the belly. When it is fastened round them they are inclined to jump around a bit, so we walk them about until they get used to it. Then the traces are put on and they are walked about again. Gradually the sleigh is brought up behind them and pulled along by hand to get them used to it. The last step is to hook their harness to the sleigh. A beginner reindeer is always harnessed alongside an old "schoolmaster" reindeer, whose presence gives him confidence and makes him realise that there is nothing to fear. In no time at all the youngsters become old hands at it.

Not surprisingly, there is a limited call for reindeer harness in this country and even in Norway, a traditional reindeer-keeping country, nobody makes collars these days because nobody harnesses reindeer any more. Fortunately, Mr Utsi brought some with him in the early days and we chanced upon somebody down south, a maker of husky sledges, who made a reindeer sledge for us one year out of ash and at the same time copied Mr Utsi's collars. We had another stroke of luck with the leather parts of the harness. While we were at a local fair in Inverness with a couple of reindeer a little lad started chatting to us. He told us that his family had just moved up from the south of England and that his father was a harness-maker. He said he would ask him to give us a ring. He did, and since then he has made all our sets of Christmas harness. They have little morris-dancer-type bells on top and look fantastic.

Christmas sleighs are not easy to come by either. The first one used by Mr Utsi was a Lappish vehicle known as a pulka, which looks a bit like a canoe. Since it was designed only for use on snow, Mr Utsi had to put wheels on it to make it go which made it look even more peculiar – not the sort of thing one normally associates with Santa Claus. When Alan became involved in Christmas events, after taking on the job of herdsman in the late 'seventies, he used something similar. Then we built a sort of chipboard sleigh and painted it red and white, but that self-destructed as soon as it got wet. Someone built us a replacement which looked a bit like a bathtub, though at least it lasted well.

Then Alan was asked to take some reindeer to Shepperton Studios to do a TV commercial. The sleigh which the property men had provided, attached to mock harness because the reindeer were not required to move, was a great big green object with curly bits, made of chipboard and with a wonderful gold painted border. It had no wheels and, being a prop, was painted on one side only. Alan, however, could see that it had potential. So at the end of the shoot he asked the props men what they were going to do with it. Throw it on the tip, they said.

Alan asked if he could have it, they said yes, so he piled it into the van with the reindeer, brought it home and it became our Christmas sleigh for many years.

The paintwork always deteriorated during the summer and it was my job to refurbish it ready for the round of Christmas events. One year I was busy with the paintbrush when somebody came to the door. I popped out of the garage for a few minutes and returned to find that our son, Alex, who was three at the time, had completely encased the hair of his eighteen-month-old sister in green gloss paint. Fiona was a beautiful blonde baby. When I saw the hideous mess her brother had made of her I had visions of having to shave her head. I am not usually an emotional person but on that occasion I burst into tears. In desperation I rang somebody up the road to ask what to do but she had no idea either. In the end I washed it out with white spirit. Goodness knows what it did to her head.

The big green sleigh lasted for several years and did a good few Christmas events. It was shaped in such a way that we could turn it on its end and tuck it into the lorry and put the reindeer in behind it. The trouble is that when you keep handling sleighs like that they eventually fall to pieces. The green one was helped on its way when Alan and I did our first Christmas season as owners of the Reindeer Company. One of the venues booked it but said they wanted to lengthen it and could they have it early to convert it. I would never dream of doing it now, but in those days I was so naive that I let them have it beforehand.

When we went to do the event the sleigh certainly looked very impressive but on closer inspection we discovered that they had only attached the extension with bits of metal and it was not very secure. Later, while we were at our final event at Grantown, which is one of our favourites, we were going up the high street, Alan leading the reindeer with the sleigh and Father Christmas with his sack, when the inevitable happened. Children have an awful habit of running along behind and jumping on to the back of the sleigh. Nowadays I am very quick to chase them off but on that occasion a group of ten-year-olds leapt on and the back of the sleigh promptly fell off. It rather spoilt the effect of Santa's grand progress up the street. I was so cross with the kids that I made them carry the broken section up the street behind us. So that was the end of the elongated sleigh and of the rest of it for that matter.

After that we decided to go for something a bit more compact, more attractive and generally more in keeping with the reindeer, who are such handsome animals, with lovely colouring. All our current sleighs were made by a friend called Beads. Beads turned up at Reindeer House one day out of the blue and is still here. He is a carpenter and builds things for us around the house. He has made some wonderful sleighs in different tones of wood, beautifully crafted and a joy to look at.

We need several sleighs these days because we run three teams of reindeer. After we had been nipping around the country doing Father Christmas and Santa's Grotto and so on for a couple of years we had a phone call from a farmer called John Richardson from Kielder in Northumberland. John had been watching a programme on TV called *The Reindeer Man*, a documentary about Mr Utsi made by the BBC back in 1975. It is repeated quite regularly and every time it appears we invariably receive the odd letter from people wanting to be a reindeer keeper, not realising that the film was made twenty years ago. One day I must get around to asking the BBC to update the postscript which says that Mr Utsi has since died and the position of the herd is unknown, or words to that effect.

In the case of John Richardson, he was not asking to become a keeper but wanting to buy a reindeer for his hill farm which he was opening to the public. I explained that we did not sell reindeer but invited him to come up to see us for a chat anyway. He and his wife, Shirley, duly made the trip, which turned out to be more adventurous than any of us had imagined. Torrential rain had caused the Spey to break its banks. The children could not go to school for a week and when John and Shirley arrived they had to wade through thigh-deep water to reach us. It was obvious straight away that John had a good eye for livestock, so we hit on the idea of letting him hire some reindeer. He did that very successfully for two summers. It was a great attraction for visitors to his farm and the reindeer came back fat as butter.

At the end of the second summer we asked John and Shirley if they would consider running a team of Christmas reindeer for us. They accepted, I organised the bookings, they came and collected the reindeer. They attended one set of venues, we went to another. It is always difficult to fit in all the people who want reindeer in the lead-up to Christmas because they invariably want them on a Saturday. This way we could be in two different places on the same weekend. A couple of years later I thought that we could probably run a third team, so we asked some friends, Rosie and Henry Humphries, down in South Wales, if they would be interested. They thought it was a great idea so now we have three.

We intend to leave it at that. What we would never do is to go rushing round the country all the year round to do things. I had a letter not long ago from a hotel wanting us to give sleigh rides at Easter, of all things. I said no. I will not do anything after Christmas. I do not believe that reindeer should spend their lives in captivity like that. I only justify the things we do with them because for the rest of the year they live a natural life up on the hill.

Running teams of Christmas reindeer is certainly hard

work, but we do have some entertaining times. On one occasion we were asked to provide reindeer for a Santa Claus photocall in mid-August, which seemed a trifle early. But we agreed to have the reindeer ready when the crew arrived at the Reindeer Centre. Crackle, making his modelling debut, was selected for the job, together with Milligan, a past master at this game and the nearest thing to an animated cuddly toy that you could imagine. Although reindeer do not mind being stroked, as a rule they do not relish someone wrapping their arms around their necks. But Milligan is so easy going that he will tolerate people lolling all over him. It is doubtful whether he actually enjoys it, but he certainly never remonstrates. His only drawback is that he has a bad habit of casting his antlers early on in the Christmas season. August presented no problems! We chose Crackle to accompany him because as a mature breeding bull he had grown a lovely big set of antlers and it was still early enough in the month for him not to have begun to strip the velvet from them. Milligan was there as a good example to show him how he should behave. Santa got togged up inside Reindeer House while we caught Milligan and Crackle in the paddock and led them round to meet their master.

I have seen some Santas in my time but this one really took the biscuit. Wearing a synthetic suit from top to toe, complete with shiny plastic face, fixed grin and a hat which could only flop one way, he was seven feet tall and about three feet wide. When he spoke I nearly wet myself. Santa's own voice had been completely distorted through some kind of electronic voice box, resulting in a sort of computerised voice. The whole scene was positively macabre: Santa had lost all semblance of jolliness and tangibility. Certainly in the eyes of an impressionable three-year-old called Calum, whose mum Liz was leading Milligan, he was definitely not someone to be trusted.

Calum took one look at the red and white monster, scuttled indoors, and did not re-emerge until he was sure the coast was clear.

So much for the "elf-like fellow" in charge of Prancer, Dancer and co. What completely floored us was the fact that Santa so totally dwarfed the reindeer. The little chaps could not possibly have pulled this outsized gentleman through the sky on Christmas Eve. The producers saw that we had a point there, at least, so it was decided that Santa should kneel down, with one reindeer on each side and the "extras" around the back. This was fine until Santa had to get up. Rather like a knight in armour, he was pretty well immobile and had to be hauled to his feet by a team of helpers.

While they were posing our assistant, Liz, noticed a hole in Santa's hat.

"Is that where your voice comes out of?" she asked.

"No," explained Santa. "That's an air vent. The suit has a fan inside it to keep me cool."

Well, all I can say is that it was not a particularly effective fan. Anyone foolhardy enough to wear that suit needed a strong heart and a liking for tropical rain forests. When he eventually emerged from his costume he was sweating like a pig. It turned out that the suit had been made by the people who make the models for *Spitting Image* and cost four and a half thousand pounds. To cap it all, the producers were convinced that this was the image we should be projecting at Christmas and that it was what the children wanted. Young Calum was apparently the exception to the rule.

We have come across many different images of Father Christmas during our travels – none of them, thankfully, along the same macabre lines as the electronic monster. Not everyone who portrays the traditional Santa Claus, however, could be said to be a natural for the role. All too often it is the assistant manager of the shopping-centre who is dragged in, with evident reluctance, to put on an ill-fitting costume. With his suit trousers all too visible, and a disastrous beard attached, more or less, by a piece of elastic, it is scarcely surprising that Santa's "Ho, ho, ho"s come out sounding so self-conscious – if, indeed, they come at all. No wonder many a Santa's beard gets yanked by a suspicious child.

The local Aviemore children have been much luckier with their Father Christmas. For many years the Aviemore Centre had its own resident Santa, a local man named George Sweeney, who grew a white beard specifically for the job. During Alan's early years with the reindeer many of the Christmas events used the Aviemore Santa. One involved doing a *Jim'll Fix It*, with George in the starring role. A young lad from Elgin had written to Jimmy Savile asking for Father Christmas and his reindeer to visit his house. The lad was the son of a distillery manager and the family lived on site – such a setting would have made it an attractive proposition for any film crew. We filmed the first part at the Aviemore Centre: Santa waking up, harnessing up the reindeer, getting into his sleigh and setting off. Then we all de-robed, put the reindeer and the sleigh into a horsebox and set off with the crew to Elgin.

The boy's mother had been well primed, ensuring that he was back from school on time with a friend in tow. It was to be a complete surprise. We harnessed up the reindeer out of sight and when all was set the cameras rolled and Santa was delivered in person to the front door of the house. Santa alighted from the sleigh and knocked on the door. When the little boy appeared he was totally taken aback. It had all worked to perfection – at least, so it seemed to my unprofessional eye. But the producer wanted a re-run because there had been a certain amount of confusion when Santa spoke to the lad and his friend and handed over a present. The boy's reaction had apparently not been good enough. So the door was shut, Santa rang again and the young lad had to feign surprise. The film crew went away satisfied. Jim had certainly "fixed it". But I could not help feeling what a shame it was they could not rest with the boy's natural reaction.

It reminded me of the time Alan and I were asked to attend the Anglican Cathedral in Liverpool to deliver Santa to a party being thrown by a television company for under-privileged children, accompanied by their parents or guardians. The reindeer were to pull the sleigh through the Cathedral, ending up at the children's party where Santa would give out presents. It was obvious by the time we were called in that it had already been a long day: the excitement and excesses had caught up with the majority of the children. Songs, sung half-heartedly, had to be repeated for the benefit of the cameras. Shots of celebrities talking to the children required retakes. We came away feeling that it had not really been a party for the children at all.

People often ask me if our own children still believe in the legend when they must have seen so many variations on the Santa Claus theme. I think that as far as they are concerned the Father Christmases they see with us are all pseuds, playing the game for children younger than themselves. The real thing is confined to Christmas Eve.

One Christmas Eve we were waiting at one of our local hotels with the reindeer all harnessed up ready for an event. It was a clear night and just as the pretend Father Christmas was getting ready for the off an aeroplane flew overhead very high, so that you could not hear it but could only see its lights flashing against the starry night sky.

With a stroke of inspiration Alan pointed it out to the children, saying, "There he goes, can you see the lights flashing on his sleigh?"

They have never forgotten it. To this day Fiona still says, "And I could hear the bells jingling on the sleigh." It was such a magical moment that at times, when the children recall it, it almost makes me believe in the magic of Christmas myself.

When Alex and Fiona were about seven and six years old, someone asked if we would take a couple of reindeer to their house in Rothiemurchus on Christmas Eve to give their three-year-old son his presents. They were a Norwegian family and Scandinavians usually receive and open their presents on Christmas Eve. It was a wonderful scene. The house was like a fairy-tale cottage. We had to walk up a dark, wooded lane, leading the reindeer and carrying lanterns. The husband was kitted out as Father Christmas, with Alex and Fiona accompanying him dressed as elves. The children played their roles out to the full and delighted in pretending to the little boy. I did wonder then if this might make them have doubts about the whole Father Christmas story – if it did, they never let on.

Not all Christmas events go as smoothly as that. One year a camera crew came up to do a shoot and found us playing around on the forest road behind the house with two of our Christmas reindeer, Keith and Albert. There was a lot of snow and we had been trying to do what the Lapps do: ski behind the reindeer. The problem was that we always train our reindeer to follow us at a slow pace, and now we wanted them to run in front and pull us. They were pretty hopeless at it because they were used to being led everywhere. When the TV crew turned up we decided to have Santa (played by George Sweeney) on his sledge being pulled down the snow-covered road.

Now George was a wonderful Santa and had done many events with us, but he had always been nervous of the reindeer and was immediately suspicious of the lack of control, no brakes on the sleigh and no one to stop the reindeer. However, we managed to get him into the sleigh, to which we had harnessed Albert, and sent them off down the slope towards the cameras. Albert, who had begun to get the idea by this time, ambled off down the slope in fine style. Until, that is, he got to the halfway mark and suddenly saw all the people standing at the bottom. With no warning he screeched to a halt. The sleigh went swinging past him and poor George, a look of sheer horror on his face, went flying out into the snow. We could not persuade George to do another take and I have a feeling that his dramatic exit was never seen on TV.

Nowadays we get fewer people like George playing Santa, at least at the big shopping-centres, and more and more celebrities. Last year at one event we had Saturday morning TV's Mr Motivator. I felt very sorry for him. It was a freezing cold day in Hartlepool and although he was wearing more than just his Lycra suit, he was absolutely frozen. He shivered his way round the streets on the sleigh and could hardly wait to get to the shopping-centre which he was due to open. He was very good, though, and really earned his money, visiting all the shops and then doing a work out for the public. Not all celebrities – I mention no names! – are as keen on giving value for money. There are also those who get very miffed if you fail to recognise them. Alan and I are not always too good at this because we have so little time to watch television, and often the public ignore them, too, because they are far more interested in the reindeer.

As we found in the sleigh-in-the-snow episode, reindeer can screech to a halt much quicker than you would expect. And they learn quickly, too, how to do particular shots. One of our funniest experiences was taking Keith and Wally to do some filming for a proposed simulator sleigh ride. The idea was that children would sit in Father

Christmas's seat in the simulator, and see Mother Christmas in front of them, driving the reindeer, and the backs of the reindeer and their antlers. Mother Christmas would drive them off down the hill to meet Father Christmas. I do not know whether the simulator ever came on to the market but it did seem a good idea for Christmas.

It was one of those situations where we could not lead the reindeer so we had to work them from behind, using reins at the side. All the reindeer had to do was pull the sleigh down a slope and stop at the bottom. We rehearsed it a few times and Keith and Wally soon had it sussed. Off they would go and as soon as they saw Santa appear they would jam on the brakes. No problem. However, when we saw the final take, it included something we had not rehearsed: halfway down dear old Wally had decided to raise his tail and produce some droppings. There they were, emerging for everyone to see, captured as it were for posterity.

These Christmas events have certainly come a long way since Mr Utsi's time. Who would have thought that one day we should be running a small fleet of purpose-built sleighs drawn by reindeer in smart leather harness. The traditional Sami reindeer harness consisted simply of a wooden collar, worn round the neck, with a rope attached to the bottom that then passed between the reindeer's legs and attached to the front of the sleigh. There were no traces, as we have today, and one could hardly blame the reindeer for misbehaving whenever the rope between their legs touched them.

The Christmas reindeer that Alan worked with when he first became a herdsman had been trained to pull a sleigh in this way. They really only tolerated the few local Christmas events they were required to do, and like a couple of misbehaving children seemed incapable of standing patiently while being harnessed up. Nevertheless they did end up pulling some well-known celebrities. In fact, in the case of a reindeer called Lad, it cured him of pulling Santa Claus for ever.

Alan, on one of his first Christmas events away from home, was asked to take a reindeer to Southampton to be filmed for television. The transport down consisted of a Land-Rover and trailer, which made the 700-mile journey very slow indeed – enough to put anyone off Christmas events for life. Lad was duly harnessed to the sleigh, and along came Santa. What no one had mentioned was the fact that Santa was none other than the wrestler, Big Daddy. Twenty-six stone of human flesh was well outside the normal range of duties for a sleigh-pulling reindeer. Poor Lad performed to the best of his ability but clearly he did not forget how heavy Santa could be. When he was next asked to perform, on Christmas Eve at one of our local hotels, he decided to get his own back. He went on strike. Nothing would persuade him to budge and in the end Santa had to alight, ignominiously, from the sleigh and carry the big sack of presents himself. This particular Santa, a rather nervous chap, promptly dropped the sack, scattering presents everywhere. Lad had taken his revenge and who could blame him?

CHAPTER TWO

Why Reindeer?

I am always being asked how I came to be involved with reindeer. I can only say that it seems to have been fate – for both Alan and me. I spent a wonderfully happy childhood in rural Hertfordshire, where my father was the local doctor in a long-established village practice. His parents were both doctors and his brother, too, was a doctor in the same practice. My mother was loving and caring, always there to solve problems and care for us when we were ill; and although my father was a busy GP he had a wealth of other interests, which were centred on sailing and natural history and in which I, my older sister and my two older brothers were encouraged to share. My sister and I had a series of ponies to look after and ride, there were always dogs everywhere and I had a pet rat called Sleepy. He was, too! In a way, I suppose, the house revolved around animals.

An avid birdwatcher, my father had spent much of his early life in the company of a local keeper in Hertfordshire, studying birdsong and wildlife. Later he developed a particular interest in the muntjac, the smallest member of the deer family. Muntjac were introduced into the south of England at the turn of the century by the Duke of Bedford for his deer park at Woburn Abbey. They are so small that they soon escaped and starting spreading out and breeding in the neighbouring countryside. My father began to study them and in due course people got to know about his interest and would bring injured ones for him to look after. Usually they had been in road accidents and the majority had to be put down. But he did manage to save some. I remember a little fawn whose leg had been mangled in a combine harvester. We called her Ivy and brought her up on the bottle. She slept in the house until she was big enough to go outside in a pen, then we found her a mate for company. We had another one later who was lame and known as Hoppy.

As time went on my elder brother, following in the family tradition, went to university to read medicine and became a doctor. So did my sister. When my turn came I announced that I wanted to be a zoologist. My father was appalled. He could not believe that anyone wanted to be something as useless as a zoologist, which seemed very strange given his great interest in natural history. I was most upset but stuck to my guns and in due course went to Bristol to read my chosen subject, make lots of friends and play hockey up to international level. But, having got my degree, what was I going to do with it? My father's point exactly! I did not relish the thought of more studying for postgraduate qualifications, so decided to pull out of the system and do something completely different.

I had heard about the reindeer in the Cairngorms and during my last year at university I decided to write to the owner of the herd, Dr Lindgren, to ask if I could work for her as a volunteer during the summer. Our paths had actually crossed some years earlier when she came one Christmas as guest speaker to my father's local natural history society. I would have been about fourteen or fifteen at the time. I remember the front door of our home, Bridge Cottage, opening and this huge figure – she stood well over six feet and was built in proportion – sweeping in in full evening dress. Even my father was a trifle overawed. He made suitable welcoming noises and hoped the bad weather would not put people off turning out for the talk. "I do hope not," she replied sternly, clearly implying that a little wintry weather in Britain was as nothing compared with the Scandinavian winters she was used to.

When she received my letter asking for a job she summoned me to meet her at her house near Cambridge. It was quite a daunting experience. The interior of the house was gloomy and she was very much on ceremony. I was given a thorough interrogation. At the end of it she announced that I could help the keeper on a voluntary basis during the summer, though something told me that it was more of a mole-in-the-camp-type job. Little did she (or I) know that in sending me to work with her reindeer keeper, Alan Smith, she was sending me to meet my future husband.

Dr Lindgren was a great correspondent. She enjoyed both receiving and writing letters and, although her handwriting was well nigh indecipherable, it was worth persevering with because her letters were always packed with snippets of information, gossip and personal views on life. Once I had been accepted to go up to Reindeer House she plied me with entertaining correspondence filled with details of the goings-on up there: who the neighbours were, why I should not hang my smalls outside on the clothes line, and why most people who went to work at Reindeer House became megalomaniacs. She also dropped frequent thinly veiled hints that I could become the full-time keeper if I wanted (relations between Alan and his employer were somewhat fraught at that period). Had I known then what the life of a reindeer keeper involved I might well have been frightened off.

It was the summer of 1981. The time came to go north and my mother lent me her car as I had to return home temporarily after the first week to attend my sister's wedding. I set off alone on the 500-mile journey. Reindeer House. In my mind's eye I saw a large, rambling shooting lodge, perched on some remote hillside. My vision could hardly have been more wide of the mark. Reindeer House is a relatively modern bungalow, built of stone in 1960 and nestling in the midst of a small Forestry Commission community across the road from a thriving campsite. I arrived to find the house unoccupied. What, no welcoming party? Slightly dismayed, I wandered round the back and asked a neighbour whether the reindeer keeper was about.

"Oh, he'll be away fishing down at the loch," came the reply. "But you can just let yourself in, the door's always open."

And sure enough, the door was unlocked. I went in and was confronted by chaos. I tend to live in chaos myself, but this was *serious* chaos. To be fair, the keeper's room was being redecorated, but I did not know that at the time and it slightly threw me to see so much junk everywhere, stacked to the ceiling. Dr Lindgren had apparently insisted on choosing the new colour for her keeper's room herself: coral pink. Very appropriate! Alan told me later that he managed to persuade the painters to put an extra gallon of white in it to tone it down.

From an inner room there came a frantic yapping noise. I opened the door to be greeted by a very small, very hairy terrier, who was clearly delighted to see me and proceeded to follow me as I explored the rest of the house. In need of a little reassurance, I decided to ring home to tell my mother I had arrived. I found the telephone, eventually, lurking on the wall in a cupboard in the hall (put there, I discovered later, to make things so uncomfortable that no one would want to settle down to a long, expensive conversation). As bad luck would have it, at the very time I rang home Alan was trying to call Reindeer House to see if I had arrived. On hearing the engaged tone he immediately assumed that I was on the phone to Dr Lindgren, reporting his absence. Dr Lindgren had apparently given him the impression that I was forty years old and built like a tank. I think he was rather dreading his first encounter with me.

It transpired that he was not fishing on the loch at all but had gone to Aberdeen for the day with his friends. When he eventually returned and I introduced myself he eyed me in a very guarded manner. But I was young and quite open and friendly and when he said later that he had some reindeer to attend to I said that was fine and toddled along with him. The first reindeer I ever met was called Eidart. Like most other people, I was surprised at how small she was. Alan decided that Eidart and her calf, who were down in the pen beside the house, should go back out on to the hill. It was a beautiful June evening and Eidart, who was a very willing reindeer, trotted eagerly along on her halter with her month-old calf in tow. The two-mile walk up the hill to the rest of the herd was my indoctrination into reindeer herding. And if this was reindeer herding, it certainly beat the pants off the prospect of life as a suburban housewife. Afterwards, when we got chatting, Alan confessed that he had only laid on this little exercise to see what I was really like. Dr Lindgren had apparently told him that I was "a very strong person" and I think it came as a pleasant surprise to find someone friendly and of his own age.

I went down south to my sister's wedding and returned to Reindeer House, as arranged, for the rest of the summer. Alan and I got on famously. I helped him with the reindeer on the hill, wrote the daily diaries, took visitors to see the herd, tried to keep the management happy and, supposedly at any rate, kept the house clean. The combination of breathtaking scenery, friendly reindeer and good company soon persuaded me that my future lay in the great outdoors. So when the autumn came I decided, to Dr Lindgren's considerable discomfiture, to stay on. Instantly I became a "hussy" in her eyes. She regarded me as a spanner in the works, even suggesting to my parents that they should "remove their daughter from the north". I think what worried her most was the possibility of my tempting Alan away from the Highlands of Scotland to the bright lights of the south. She and Alan might not always have seen eye to eye, but she clearly respected him and valued the work he did and was afraid that if he left, the whole enterprise would grind to a halt.

In the meantime Alan and I had a whale of a time. Life carried on very much as normal, except that I became an unofficial resident. It was all harmless really and quite a laugh at times. While official visitors were coming in through the front door of Reindeer House, I would be making a hasty exit through the keeper's window (good job it was a bungalow!). Answering the telephone was never a good idea because it would invariably be Dr Lindgren at the other end.

On one memorable occasion I hid in a cupboard with my dog Truffle while guests were passing through the house. Truffle and Alan's little terrier, Fly, the dog I had met the day I arrived, had taken an instant dislike to each other and were constantly scrapping. If you have ever played hide and seek with dogs around, you will know how quickly they give the game away. On this occasion Fly was most intrigued by my being incarcerated in the cupboard with Truffle and insisted on standing guard outside. Alan explained Fly's behaviour away to the guests by saying there must be a mouse in there. Cheek! When Dr Lindgren arrived for her regular visits I used to take a tent and camp out on the hill with the reindeer.

All this French-farce behaviour finally came to an end in the summer of 1983 when Alan and I were married. It was a memorable occasion which brought Alan's entire family south of the border for the first time in their lives. Alan's grandfather took his shepherd's crook with him –

just in case. When we returned to Reindeer House the keeper's room became the sitting-room and the guest room the married quarters. I immediately became acceptable again to Dr Lindgren, and Alan and I set about running the herd as an official duo.

Alan's background could not have been more different from mine, which is probably why we hit it off so well. His father was a hill farmer from Ballater, just over the hill from where we are now. The family, mother, father and six children, of whom Alan was the oldest, lived in a bothy with no running water, no toilet and no electricity. When Alan was fourteen his father, who had always been interested in deer, decided to get a job as a deer stalker, so they all moved up to Lord Thurso's estate in Caithness. There they were based in a god-forsaken place fifteen miles up a sand-track road in the middle of endless moorland.

Technically Alan was still at school, but by all accounts he spent very little time there. Instead he would be out stalking red deer with his father or grouse beating on the moors. On one occasion when he did turn up at school the teacher asked him where he had been and why he had come back. He said he had been out cutting peats but had come back to take his exams. He was advised to go back to cutting peats.

As a teenager he did various jobs, working on the farm and helping his father as a ghillie. But he soon realised that working with his father on a permanent basis was not going to be viable and started looking for employment elsewhere. Then one morning his mother, who reads the local paper from cover to cover every day, including the advertisements, spotted something she thought might suit him. Mr Utsi and Dr Lindgren were advertising for a reindeer keeper. She badgered Alan to ring up and in due course he got an interview. As luck would have it he was able to give as his referee Commander Carmichael, who owned the neighbouring estate to the one where his father worked. Alan had done some stalking for him and it turned out that the Commander knew Dr Lindgren very well. Alan got the job immediately.

Accompanied by his little dog Fly, Alan moved into Reindeer House in the November of 1978. He was eighteen, had never seen a reindeer before (he expected them to look like goats) and had no idea what he was supposed to do. He had imagined that the work would involve jumping on a tractor, driving out to a field and chucking bales of hay to the herd. How wrong can you be! His first day saw him walking with the temporary keeper to spy for reindeer, who were scattered over a wide area out on the hill. Now Alan is a true hillman, with a very good eye for anything that moves, and quickly spotted some reindeer, miles away, which had eluded his companion. They were several hours' walk away. The following day he set out, found them and brought them back nearer to base. When he rang his employer to say that the reindeer had been found, all Mr Utsi had to say was, "You must have a very good pair of binoculars."

Despite his off-hand attitude though, he must have realised at once that in Alan he had at last found a potentially professional herdsman, someone to replace the succession of people who had come to Reindeer House with no experience of hillwork and no aptitude for handling reindeer. By all accounts none of Alan's predecessors had stayed long. They were never exactly fired, they simply moved on, unable to cope either with the work or the somewhat difficult herdsman/employer relationship. Apparently Mr Utsi would tell them to do one thing and Dr Lindgren another. They ended up thoroughly confused and, all too often, more than a little irritated. Young though he was, Alan was diplomatic enough not to argue. He just agreed with everything he

43

was told and then got on with the job in his own way, doing what he felt was best for the reindeer.

Alan only met Mr Utsi once, when he was asked to go down to his Cambridge home. Mr Utsi was already ill by that time and could no longer make the long journey north to visit his beloved reindeer. For Alan, who had never been south of Perth before, the journey was quite an undertaking, travelling by train from Aviemore to London and then finding his way up to Cambridge. Mr Utsi and Dr Lindgren seemed quite impressed when he made a prompt arrival. Alan spent a week driving Dr Lindgren about, on her insistence visiting a dentist to get his teeth attended to, and running sundry errands.

One day when he returned to the house Mr Utsi was missing. They found him, ill though he was, at the bottom of the garden with his shotgun. He had just felled a hare in the adjoining field with one of the longest shots with a 12-bore that Alan had ever seen. Even Alan was impressed. He did not learn a great deal about reindeer from Mr Utsi in the short time he knew him but he was sent off to the Lappish-style hut in the garden to see if he could turn his hand to any of the traditional crafts associated with reindeer herding, such as carving antlers. Alan felt that he was just being tested, to see whether he had any sense – Mr Utsi's kind of sense, that is – in his head.

After his week in Cambridge Alan returned to Reindeer House and prepared for his first calving. It went really well and he was congratulated by Mr Utsi on the results. Once it was over Alan went off on his holidays. By the time he returned in June Mr Utsi had died and he found himself virtually in control of the herd. Dr Lindgren (although she and Mr Utsi were married, we always knew her as Dr Lindgren) turned up the following month. It was the first time she had visited Reindeer House since Alan's arrival. She took one look at his clothes – perfectly normal cord trousers and shirts and so on – said what a mess he looked and immediately had him measured for keeper's suits: tweeds, plus fours, the lot. Whenever he went out with her and her visitors, even in the height of summer, he had to dress in his keeper's tweed suit. To cap it all, she had an awful habit of handing him her handbag to hold. Alan was remarkably stoical.

"I was her keeper and she wanted me to play the part," he said. "The visitors probably thought that's how everybody up here dressed. Anyway none of them knew me, so I didn't mind."

Apart from being heavily into Elvis Presley when I first met him (people in the Highlands are always about ten years behind everybody else) Alan was chiefly interested in wildlife in general and reindeer in particular, with whom he clearly had a huge rapport. But perhaps the thing I admired most about him was how incredibly in tune he was, and still is, with the hills. We used to trek for miles and while I never knew where I was, he would never ever get lost. He never takes a map with him, but he always knows exactly where he is. He used to tell me, "Always see where you are before the weather closes in. If you don't, that's how you become lost." I would still never go right into the heart of the Cairngorms without him.

In those days the reindeer were not controlled as much as we control them today and were always straying out of their designated 6,000 acres. Often it would take Alan a whole day to walk out and find the missing ones. Sometimes, if they were in a good place for grazing, he would simply leave them. The herd was only small at that time, and the neighbouring estates were on the whole very tolerant because they knew they were not a threat to the red deer or the grouse or sheep – reindeer country is a bit high for sheep anyway. And since Alan had been a deer stalker himself he was never likely to wander across their land at the wrong moment and disturb someone's sport.

With no one to teach him the finer points of reindeer herding – Dr Lindgren was an anthropologist rather than an animal-minded person – he learned the job as he went along, often the hard way. One piece of advice which both Dr Lindgren and Mr Utsi gave him proved to be very wide of the mark. Always carry a stick, they said. So he did. One day when he went to fetch the herd from the top of the hill a big bull came over and threatened him with his antlers. Hoping to drive him off, Alan struck his antlers with his walking stick. To a reindeer that meant only one thing: attack! He did, sending the stick and Alan's bag of feed flying. Somehow Alan managed to grab hold of the top of the reindeer's antlers and get himself round behind the animal's head. By twisting round and round in small circles he succeeded in steering the reindeer over to the fence, some fifty yards away, where he dived through the wire to safety.

That brought home to him the fact that to the bull reindeer a stick is a sign of aggression, the equivalent of another bull's antlers. And antlers are for fighting. The last thing you want is to appear aggressive to a bull. What he should have done was to turn away, appear subservient. Alan no longer carries a stick.

CHAPTER THREE

Mr Utsi and Dr Lindgren

M r Utsi and Dr Lindgren were what could only be described as a most unusual couple. He, short, stocky and weatherbeaten, came from a traditional Sami (Lapp) background, had spent the first fifteen years of his life herding reindeer with his family in northern Sweden, was a dab hand with a lasso and was never more at home than when striding across a mountainside in his colourful Lapp clothing. She, statuesque, elegant and given to making sweeping entrances at smart social functions, was born in Illinois into a wealthy Swedish-American banking family, became a notable Cambridge academic, lecturing in anthropology, and was a pillar of English village life.

At first sight an unlikely couple, these two remarkable characters were drawn together by a shared interest in reindeer-herding peoples and a mutual love of their equally remarkable animals. Pooling their considerable expertise, they set up the reindeer reintroduction programme in the Scottish Highlands, to which Alan and I became, in the fullness of time, the proud and happy heirs.

Sadly, I never met Mikel Utsi, and Alan knew him for a regrettably short time. But by all accounts he was a fascinating, witty, entertaining man, remembered in Scotland for his sense of fun, his constant leg-pulling, his infectious laughter and an endless repertoire of stories, many based on his adventures during the Second World War.

Mikel Nils Persson Utsi was born on May 17, 1908 in Karesuando, the second of eight sons of a well-known reindeer-owning family. He grew up with the herd, accompanying them on migration each year, living and breathing reindeer lore. During the late thirties and the Second World War years the resourceful Mikel Utsi had a varied career. He ran restaurants; he served three periods in the Swedish army and as a Swedish special constable helped rescue many hundreds of Norwegian refugees escaping from the Germans across the wild, mountainous borderland. After the war he was awarded the Freedom Medal by Norway's King Haakon.

In 1947 he married Dr Lindgren in the church at Jokkmokk in traditional Lappish style, and the couple settled near Cambridge, founding, two years later, the Reindeer Council of the United Kingdom "to encourage experiments in reindeer breeding in suitable areas in Scotland and/or overseas". During a visit to Scotland in the year of his marriage, Mr Utsi had been struck by the suitability of the Cairngorms for reindeer herding.

"Where are your reindeer?" he had asked in surprise, surveying the hillsides with their ample supply of mosses and lichens, the natural food of these tundra animals. Convinced that reindeer could thrive and provide a welcome source of meat for the people of post-war Britain, he set about trying to establish a programme of reintroduction.

No one is quite sure when reindeer died out in Scotland. According to the Orkneyinga Saga they were still being hunted in Caithness, alongside red deer, as late as the twelfth century. Some experts, however, are doubtful that they survived the warming up of the climate following the last Ice Age, thousands of years before. I like to think that the Vikings may have brought some with them in their long boats. Whatever the truth of the matter, they had certainly died out at some point, either from over-hunting or climatic changes or a combination of both.

In recent times various attempts have been made to reintroduce reindeer to Scotland and northern England. The Duke of Atholl imported fourteen to his estate in the 1790s, but some died on the rough crossing from Archangel and more were lost on their way north from Leith. Only three eventually arrived at the Atholl estate and they did not survive. Sir Henry Liddell had similar misfortune with five Swedish reindeer imported into Northumberland. After a promising start, when they successfully reared some young, they perished from a form of foot-rot, attributed to over-rich pasture.

In 1816 Robert Traill introduced a male and two females from Archangel to his farm at Wideford, near Kirkwall, on the mainland of Orkney. However, they all died during their first winter. Inappropriate food and the damp climate were blamed, although there are suggestions that they were deliberately allowed to die as they were found to be unsuitable for their intended purpose.

Finally, in the Forest of Mar on the southern side of the Cairngorms, the Earl of Fife tried to establish some around 1820. One beast found its way to the high tops of the Cairngorms, perfect reindeer country. But it was not soon enough and it, too, died.

Mr Utsi was determined that his bid would be successful and in the fullness of time he managed to gain a permit from the Ministry of Agriculture to import twenty-five animals. On April 7, 1952 eight Swedish mountain reindeer, the most that could be accommodated on the deck of the only available freight boat, arrived in Glasgow from Narvik.

The report of the newly formed Reindeer Company Ltd describes how the reindeer, two three-year-old bulls, two two-year-old females, three yearling female calves and one four-year-old draught ox (ox is the term for a gelded male reindeer) had to endure a rough four-day crossing but seemed to cope well, using their wonderfully developed "snow feet" to great effect to keep their balance.

The reindeer were accompanied on their journey by Mr Utsi and his cousin, Nikolaus Labba, who continued to assist Mr Utsi for the first year. Poor Mr Utsi, ever attentive to the animals' needs, fared rather less well on the journey than they did: he was gored in the left eye by an antler as he was feeding them in their crates during a gale and arrived in Scotland sporting a jaunty eyepatch.

On arrival the reindeer had to go into quarantine, where various precautionary health tests were made and treatment given for warbles. The larvae of the warble fly penetrate the animal's skin and appear as small, painful lumps on the back. Some of the larvae had died under the reindeer's skin, resulting in painful sores that had to be operated on. One light-coloured calf had been particularly badly afflicted. It was six and a half weeks before the reindeer could be introduced to their new home near Aviemore and during that time the light-coloured calf sadly died.

The land provided for the Utsis' experiment was a 300-acre enclosure on the lower slopes of the Cairngorms, generously made available by the late Colonel J. P. Grant, of Rothiemurchus. Doubts were expressed at the time about the suitability of the site as a summering ground for the herd, on account of the numerous biting insects, and Mr Utsi must have known right from the beginning of the enterprise that more suitable summer pasture would have to be found in due course. But it was a start.

Part of the land was already enclosed, although before the reindeer could be turned out on it a further two miles of fencing had to be erected. Nothing daunted, Mr Utsi set to with a will, ably assisted by two volunteer undergraduates, one from Oxford and one from Cambridge, and various local helpers.

Eventually the seven surviving reindeer were delivered to their new quarters. The inclusion in this first group of a non-breeding gelded male may seem somewhat incongruous, when the whole point of the exercise was for the reindeer to multiply. However Sarek, the four-year-old draught ox, was very much a symbol of all that Mr Utsi stood for and was attempting to achieve.

He was not reintroducing reindeer to Scotland as a wild animal but bringing them in to be herded and managed in the traditional Lappish way. An animal like Sarek was an integral part of this lifestyle: the beast of burden and the decoy or leader traditionally used by reindeer herders. Indeed, Sarek led the herd for many years. It must have been very much the end of an era for Mr Utsi when he finally went missing, presumed dead, at the ripe old age of sixteen. As Mr Utsi said: "Perhaps he has gone rest."

After seeing the first small group of reindeer settled into their new enclosure, Mr Utsi set off again for Sweden later in the year to select another group, this time of forest reindeer. Unlike their mountain-bred cousins, forest reindeer are seldom herded and so are much less approachable and it took all of his lassoing skills for Mr Utsi to acquire his desired quota.

The sea crossing, which took seven days this time instead of the usual four, was the stormiest of the season. Yet the reindeer, protected in their crates by large tarpaulins, again seemed little troubled by the weather. After four anxious weeks in quarantine in Glasgow, Mr Utsi was able to accompany them – one bull and nine females – on the final nine-hour stage of their journey by road to Aviemore. The Company's report records that "at 1 a.m. the reindeer were released to graze in their fenced Reserve. After some cautious reconnoitring the forest reindeer approached the pioneer mountain reindeer. In a few hours the two groups had formed a small herd."

The following February Mr Utsi gained a couple more additions to the herd when he was happily reunited with Alta, a reindeer he had presented to London Zoo in 1951. The zoo was finding the cost of feeding their reindeer (on lichen imported from Iceland) too expensive and decided to offer Alta back to her original owner to run with the Scottish herd. The Reindeer Company accepted, buying another zoo-bred female at the same time. Mr Utsi is probably the only person to have travelled north on the night express from Euston in the company of two reindeer.

Things were by no means easy at the beginning of the reintroduction programme. Mr Utsi faced many setbacks as he struggled to establish the herd in its new environment. During their first year at Rothiemurchus six of the original two groups of imported reindeer died, the mountain type faring rather worse than the forest type. The stress of the long journey and close confinement in quarantine, which Mr Utsi always felt put the animals under tremendous strain, had evidently taken its toll, though other factors were also involved: one of the forest animals who died during the winter had almost certainly been injured by a motor vehicle. The reindeer were also plagued by midges, mosquitoes and flies. Numbers were bolstered when the first Scottish calving, in May 1953, produced three bull calves; but the summer that year was exceptionally wet, causing further parasite problems for the herd. Mr Utsi knew that it was imperative for the animals to be moved to higher, drier grazing if they were to thrive. When the Forestry Commission offered some 6,000 acres on the largely barren, unplantable northern slopes of Cairngorm, it put the whole experiment on a new footing. Personally, I am absolutely certain that he had his sights set on that high ground all along. From 1954 onwards the reindeer have grazed, unfenced but herded, in these far more suitable conditions. When, in the early 'seventies, the land was sold to the Highlands and Islands Development Board, becoming their Cairngorm Estate, the reindeer-grazing arrangement remained unchanged.

In April 1953 more reindeer were imported to complete the quota of twenty-five originally authorised by the Ministry of Agriculture. On this occasion Mr Utsi only had an import licence for seven, but he shipped eight over, to cover possible accidents. This, of course, caused a tremendous stir with the authorities and it was Dr Lindgren, in true diplomatic style, who had to smooth the waves. The third consignment definitely acclimatised the best, the higher ground giving the herd much-needed relief from flies and heat during the summer.

However, there was a major setback that autumn, during the rutting season, when a mature bull named Aviemore was found drowned in one of the hill lochs, his antlers tangled in wire. It must have been a tremendous blow to the project and prompted a further request from Mr Utsi for permission to bring in two new bulls from his Swedish mountain herd.

Because of his long absences from the herd while he was bringing in new consignments and overseeing them in quarantine, Mr Utsi depended heavily on the presence of a reindeer herder and he always encouraged voluntary help from outsiders keen to learn about reindeer breeding, especially after the departure of his cousin, Nikolaus Labba. Thereafter various local people applied for the post of herder. When it came to reindeer husbandry Mr Utsi drove a hard bargain, demanding one hundred per cent effort morning, noon and night. On one occasion he wanted a young herder actually to live on the hill so that he could light smudge fires to ward off insects early in the morning between June and September – something which would have been perfectly acceptable in the traditional nomadic lifestyle of the Sami people. Dr Lindgren had to intervene, suggesting a compromise in which the keeper worked a morning shift, arriving on the hill at 6 a.m. Some herders lasted a couple of years, others departed after a couple of days.

The daily task of a reindeer herder revolved around the gathering of the reindeer, herding them on the open hill and locating strays. From the beginning Mr Utsi and his helpers erected fenced areas where the herd could be held and a small hut was built down in the forest to provide shelter on wet days. Utsi's hut, as it was known, was constructed from the crates in which the reindeer had travelled and was the focal point of the whole enterprise. Reindeer could be herded down for veterinary treatment and fires could be lit in the vicinity to repel insects in summer. There was also vehicular access to the hut which meant that visitors could be driven this far before setting off on foot to see the herd. Visitors were encouraged right from the start. Mr Utsi clearly enjoyed showing off his reindeer to members of the public, though with his colourful Sami costume and heavily accented English, he may well have been more of an attraction to some people than the reindeer.

By the end of the 1950s the reindeer were beginning to find their feet and during the rut of 1959 one of the bulls took his group of females off into the hills. In his quest for them Mr Utsi had to contact gamekeepers and stalkers on neighbouring estates to enquire whether they had seen any straying on their land. One keeper whom he spoke to suspected there had been inter-breeding between the reindeer and the red deer because he had seen "one very odd-shaped pair of antlers". Another reported a definite sighting of a reindeer on his estate, but after a few drams with Mr Utsi his description changed and the sighting was not pursued. Eventually, the renegades turned up of their own accord, but thereafter Mr Utsi and his herders began to venture further afield to gather up the strays.

In October 1961 Mr Utsi was given permission to bring more reindeer into the country, this time forest reindeer from South Norway. Being semi-wild, they were badly affected by the stress of travelling and quarantine and out of the eight brought in only three survived.

It was in the early 'sixties that the ski road was built from the Glenmore Forest up the hill to a car park at nearly 2,000 ft. This greatly increased access out on to the hill and had important implications for the reindeer. The natural predator of the reindeer is the wolf, and although the ski road did not bring wolves it did bring a posse of people with their dogs, including the uncontrolled variety. Mr Utsi had a bee in his bonnet about loose dogs, and not surprisingly, for there were at least two undisputed cases of dogs causing the death of reindeer. In those early days the calving season was producing only five or six new members for the herd and any setback to its expansion was, naturally, a tremendous blow.

Loose dogs can be a very real menace to reindeer who, when panicked, may split up. Once separated from the herd, young reindeer in particular are terribly vulnerable, unable to find enough food and pining for the company of their fellows. Reindeer also heat up very quickly. Incapable of losing heat through their thick coats, they become very stressed if they are chased over long distances.

Mr Utsi's dislike of dogs was total. He went so far as to claim that reindeer would not trust anyone smelling of dogs, and they were accordingly banned from Reindeer House.

Despite this new intrusion of dogs on the hill, by the end of the 1960s the herd was showing real signs of growth.

Of the seventy reindeer present for the 1969 rutting season, nineteen were calves born the previous spring. When Scottish Television filmed a documentary, *The Reindeer Man*, in 1973, Mr Utsi must have felt that all the hard work and perseverance of the early days had at last paid off. The herd was generating small quantities of much sought-after meat and was attracting parties of visitors from far afield.

A number of young reindeer were also being sold to zoos and country parks throughout England and Scotland, notably Chester Zoo, the Norfolk Wildlife Park at Great Witchingham and the Highland Wildlife Park at Kincraig. All these establishments still have reindeer descended from the original Scottish stock imported by Mr Utsi.

In 1973 a Russian bull, Kivi, joined the herd from Whipsnade Zoo. Russian reindeer in general stand a little higher at the shoulder than Scandinavian reindeer, who average about 3ft 6in when fully grown, and the introduction of this new blood was a tremendous boost. By the summer of 1977 there were 102 reindeer in the herd, despite some culling and live sales.

Slowly but surely Mr Utsi's dream of seeing reindeer thrive in the Highlands of Scotland was coming to fruition. Although by this time his health was in decline and he was no longer able to spend time on the hills personally supervising the herd, he had been proved right in his belief that reindeer could live healthy, happy lives roaming the snow line on the Cairngorms, from which they had been missing for hundreds, perhaps thousands, of years.

His love for his reindeer is well demonstrated in a letter he wrote during the summer of 1975, when he first became very ill, to be displayed at Reindeer House:

Dear Visitors to the Reindeer

However much I might have wished to guide you, as before, to my dear reindeer, around which my thoughts are always circling, my health advisers have rescued me to this home of rest. I hope nevertheless that it will not be for too long a time. I am confident that if there is anywhere in the world that I can be restored, I am in that place.

Every morning, when you start driving up from Reindeer House, towards the reindeer in the hope of reaching them somewhere on the slopes of the Cairngorms, I think of you.

Yours devoted

Mikel Utsi

Although Mr Utsi became a British subject in 1955, he never relinquished his ties with his native people. He took an active interest in developments in his homeland and would go to great pains to brief anthropologists planning to work among the Sami people. Lappish etiquette was, and still is, a particularly important subject. He saved many a visitor from making the biggest gaffe of all: asking a Sami how many reindeer he owned.

When he was a lad in north Sweden punitive taxes were imposed on the Sami according to the size of their herds, quite apart from which the number of reindeer a family owned was a direct reflection of their wealth. Asking a Sami how many reindeer he has is tantamount to asking someone how much money they have in their bank account.

Tremendously proud of his Sami roots, he still wore, whenever he could, his traditional, colourful costume and always hanging by his bed were his reindeer-skin tunic with its colourful braid and Sami hat with its bright red pompon. In the garden of his house near Cambridge he built his own Sami kåta, the summer residence of a reindeer herder when the herds were on the move. Designed exactly on the same lines as a North American Indian wigwam, these tents could be loaded on to pack reindeer as the herders moved from place to place. Meat and fish would be hung above the central fire to be smoked. Originally made of reindeer skins, modern Sami tents are canvas. Mr Utsi must have wanted his to last because he built it of concrete. Also in his garden was an upturned boat, used as a shed and stuffed full of reindeer antlers. Mr Utsi never parted with any of his reindeer's antlers. He used a few for making into handicrafts but otherwise hoarded them like a squirrel.

Until illness finally prevented him from making the long trip north, he was a popular and instantly recognisable figure in and around Aviemore. An accomplished craftsman, he made fine carvings in bone, antler and wood. And at Christmas time he would provide reindeer to delight the local children. Above all, he loved his reindeer, knew them all by name, tended them when they were sick, fed them by hand and talked to them as if they were his friends – which they were.

By the time Alan became reindeer herder Mr Utsi was too frail to leave Cambridge. How he must have missed the day-to-day contact with his beloved reindeer. It probably made him very suspicious of young herders like Alan, which could account for the many heated telephone calls he made to Reindeer House – often one could hear Dr Lindgren's voice in the background trying to calm him down.

In his absence Alan was provided with a set of rules to follow:

THE REINDEER COMPANY LIMITED
REINDEER RESERVE ROUTINE
in the absence of Mr Utsi
originally drafted in 1971
(Instructions brought up-to-date in June 1978)

(1) Before leaving Reindeer House, spy out the nearest slopes carefully with field-glasses.

(2) Leave Reindeer House for checking the herd at 9 a.m., or, if you are taking visitors up, at 11 a.m. If reindeer are missing, someone should go up earlier.

(3) Each person doing reindeer work must carry a raincoat or other waterproof clothing, a haversack containing a bag with about 3lb of supplementary fodder, in the correct mixture (more, if the reindeer are fenced in); one packet of Ryvita; a reindeer halter; and his own picnic lunch, preferably with Thermos. A walking stick is always useful. A sharp knife is required if a reindeer has died on the hill, for skinning.

(4) An eye should be kept on the herd until most people have come down from the hills; and someone must be within reach of the reindeer until 5.30 p.m. in case a dog attacks them, or people worry the calves. (Hours are of course longer in the calving season.) If the reindeer are all right, fences should be carefully checked for weak spots.

(5) The reindeer should be kept out of sight of the ski road, ski car park and ski lift and for that reason should not be fed with the mixture or Ryvita on or near that area.

(6) If there are loose dogs about, the owner must be warned to keep the dog on a lead. One can mention

small calves in the herd or other special circumstances. If no owner can be found the dog must be taken down to Reindeer House and reported to the Forester, to the Police, or both.

(7) Visitors who are good walkers and are suitably equipped for the hill can be taken up for payment, but not people unfit, too old, or too young.

Old or young can come as far as the Kåta Shelter in the East Enclosure, to visit the nearest reindeer. Payment at the gate. No dogs are allowed inside the reindeer enclosures.

Salt licks should always be put out when the reindeer are fenced in.

M.N.P. Utsi
25 June 1978

When he died on June 30, 1979, at the age of seventy-one much of his knowledge, sadly, died with him. At the time there was much speculation as to whether the reindeer herd would even continue. But Dr Lindgren was a very determined lady and, with a young, able keeper like Alan to tend the herd on the hill, life did in fact carry on as normal.

Mr Utsi and Dr Lindgren, at first sight such an incongruous couple, formed a formidable team. Born on New Year's Day, 1905, Ethel John Lindgren was educated in Boston and by the time she was seventeen was already a seasoned traveller. At fifteen she visited Japan. At sixteen she undertook the Grand Cultural Tour of Western Europe. At seventeen she rode into Manchuria to see the inner section of the Great Wall of China.

At Newnham College, Cambridge, she took a first-class honours degree in experimental psychology. Before visiting China for a second time she passed part one of the Chinese Tripos, which she studied as a subsidiary subject, in a year. She also spoke English, Swedish, French, German and Russian as well as some Dutch, Mongol and the language of the Manchurian reindeer nomads, the Tungus.

Between 1928 and 1932 she returned to Manchuria several times to live and travel with groups of reindeer Tungus. Much of this part of Manchuria had never been surveyed and the journey to the nomads' land was along the course of the Bystraya River, itself quite incorrectly shown on Russian maps.

Dr Lindgren's expedition travelled on horseback and the inhabitants of the small reindeer Tungus' encampment which they came upon allowed them to live as nomads alongside them. When on the move the horses always travelled ahead of the reindeer so as not to frighten them. Dr Lindgren became particularly fond of a shamaness (witch doctor) called Olga. By Tungus standards Olga and her husband were prosperous, wealth being gauged by their fine herd of reindeer and good reserves of flour.

Late autumn and early winter was the squirrel-hunting season and the Tungus moved camp frequently at this time of year in order to maximise the number of squirrels they could catch. The men always walked ahead to blaze the trail and prepare a new camp site, shooting on the way. Generally, although the Tungus were clearly very flexible and there was no strict division of labour, the women were responsible for finding, catching and packing the reindeer in order to move camp.

Every pack reindeer had its own saddle and halter, which would only be transferred to another reindeer when the first one died. Everything – panniers of dry flour, kettles, crockery, squirrel carcasses, tents and babies tied in cradles – was packed on to the reindeer. The case containing shamanistic images was always placed on a white reindeer. There would be some two dozen reindeer forming a train as they set off through the forest. Extremely tame and tractable, these reindeer were an essential mode of transport for the Tungus.

On a third expedition, Dr Lindgren visited the Tungus during May and June, calving time. Now, she found, the reindeer's behaviour was quite different, as they scattered much further afield to find the first blades of grass. The reindeer were seldom required for transport at this time of year but the cows were milked and the calves tethered near the camp to accustom them to people and prevent them from taking all the cows' milk. For the Tungus summer passed in a leisurely fashion. With travelling made impossible by the heat and the swampy valleys impassable following the thaw, humans and reindeer alike relaxed around the encampment.

Although Dr Lindgren wrote her PhD thesis on *The Reindeer Tungus of Manchuria*, very little of her anthropological work has been published. I believe that the reason was her loyalty to these people and her wish to preserve their anonymity during the Communist era. She never returned to Manchuria but she did retain her interest in reindeer nomads, visiting Swedish Lapland on several occasions, which is how she came to know the Utsi family.

From 1936 to 1939 she was research fellow at Newnham. She lectured at Cambridge in social anthropology and helped to receive many war refugees. She became a British citizen in 1940 and was fiercely patriotic. She served on the Council of the Royal Anthropological Institute for twenty-eight years, and was twice a member of the Council of the Royal Geographical Society. She was also a founding fellow of Lucy Cavendish College in Cambridge, a college for mature women students. Her indomitable personality enabled her to get things done – and to mobilise others into getting things done.

From the time Alan and I came to work at Reindeer House until her death in 1988 at the age of eighty-three Dr Lindgren was, not surprisingly, a dominant force in our lives. She administered the Reindeer Company, assisted by a loyal secretary, Mrs Shreeve, from her home village of Harston, near Cambridge, but made regular sorties north to oversee the operation in person.

Reindeer House would go into a totally different gear when she was there. She always occupied the smallest bedroom in the house. She was a big woman and I think it was a deliberate ploy as she made a point of receiving people in her room. One of my jobs, which I inherited from Alan, was to take her breakfast each morning – she never cooked – and there, hanging on the back of the door, would be her wolf-skin coat. On the first night of each visit she always slept in it. I am not a person who worries overmuch about smells, but that coat really had a raunchy smell to it. On other nights she would sleep in blankets. She never put sheets on the bed. There is a tiny drawing of her on the loo door, drawn by Mr Utsi to indicate that only women should use the inside loo. The men were banished to the outside one.

From her bedroom she would organise her day, arrange lunch appointments and then return to grill us individually about the day's news. She seldom interrogated us together. She was a past master at drawing information out of others without giving anything away herself. I would have dearly loved to hear about her own exploits, her expeditions to far-flung places, but she was completely unforthcoming, clamming up or changing the subject in response to a direct question. In her unwillingness to talk about herself and her intense dislike of having her photograph taken she was quite unlike her husband.

She had met Mr Utsi while on a visit to Sweden to study the Sami people. By that time he was not as involved in

The genuine Christmas article, from Santa's specially grown
whiskers to the tips of the reindeer antlers.

Christmas duty starts in a shopping-centre service area in Basildon, Essex. Gustav wants to make sure Mackerel and Frostie are keeping up. Reindeer are sociable animals who hate being separated. Frostie is along to learn the ropes and hog the photo opportunity with Santa.

Above, Mica and Johan demonstrating their professional good nature. Below, Keith does a spot of hospital visiting and makes a young patient's day.

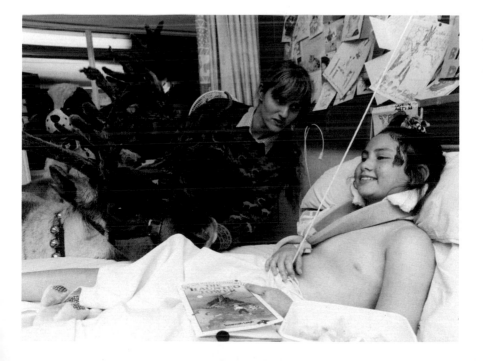

Left, the first of the herd en route from Narvik to Glasgow in 1952. Sarek was to be herd leader. Mr Utsi, for all his experience, hadn't managed to move fast enough when feeding his eight pioneers in the hold of the ship.

IF YOU CAN'T RUN
47 miles an hour
FOLLOW THe FENCE
Please

Right, Mr Utsi was a great communicator. Below, sawing off a bull's antlers is a painless process once the velvet is shed. All you need is his co-operation.

Above, feeding
Hannah out on the
hill with eight-
month-old Alex
along for the ride;
below, ten years later,
Napoleon and
friends come to the
lusher pastures of
Glenlivet.

At Glenlivet we wanted to regenerate the land for our second herd. Charlie, above left, a prime Iron-Age boar, was our chief digging machine. Middle left, Charlie and Susie's offspring – all future rooters. Below, Alan feeds the herd. The days of hill sheep are long gone here.

Above right, Fiona (aged 6) holds Beauty (aged one day) before her mother, Sorrel, died. Middle right, Beauty at two weeks is being hand-reared and thinks she's a dog. Below, she also thinks I am her mother and shadows me everywhere on the hill, here while I attempt to feed Crackle.

The calving season is around the second week in May. White cows, much prized for their magical qualities by the Sami of old, produce white calves (above). Stream with her calf Saturn, below. Female reindeer keep their antlers the longest.

reindeer herding as the rest of his family. But he was a colourful character and would have been the obvious person to show visiting anthropologists around. By this time he was probably wondering what else he could do in life and between them they must have thought up the plan to bring reindeer back to the Scottish Highlands.

Like Mr Utsi, Dr Lindgren had been married before and, like Mr Utsi, she too had a son by her first marriage. When I first became involved with the reindeer I heard a wild rumour from the local people that husband number one had died during an expedition to the Gobi desert and had been eaten by his companions, including his wife. For a while I half believed it! Later, on one of the rare occasions when Dr Lindgren confided in me, she told me that she had divorced him because he was lazy. That sounded much more plausible.

She and Mr Utsi had other things in common besides reindeer, not least their unusual personalities. Just as it would have been hard to miss the flamboyant Mr Utsi in his Sami costume so Dr Lindgren was equally difficult to overlook, not just because of her size and regal bearing but because she could and did converse on such unusual topics. No one could fail to take notice when she held court in a restaurant. She always had a good story to tell and enjoyed analysing other people. The conversation at her table was invariably so much better than anything going on around her that one always had the feeling the occupants of neighbouring tables were listening in.

She loved catching people out and watching their reactions. The classic example involved an employee of the Highlands and Islands Development Board, a young chap whom Dr Lindgren had met on a number of occasions, the HIDB being the owners of the land leased by the Reindeer Company. Various letters went to and fro between the HIDB and the lessee and, unfortunately for the young man in question, an internal memo to a fellow colleague, which included a description of Dr Lindgren, accidentally ended up in the same envelope as a letter sent to her. Nothing was said until one evening she invited this poor man to one of her dinners at a local Aviemore hotel. To his chagrin the memo was suddenly produced and the interrogation began.

We always felt her presence at Reindeer House, even when she was not there in person. She would ring up regularly demanding a blow-by-blow account of everything you had done that day and she expected you to keep detailed daily diaries. For Alan, who avoids putting pen to paper at the best of times, writing a diary was a tremendous chore that was often overlooked. Dr Lindgren would send near-unreadable letters trying to persuade him of its importance. While she was in residence, of course, the diary tended to be completed: lists of reindeer seen that day, the goings on at Reindeer House, who had been to visit and, more especially, who was staying.

Her imminent arrival would prompt a flurry of other activity, too, particularly on the domestic front: everything from washing the floor and cleaning the cooker, to throwing out burnt saucepans and replenishing the drinks cabinet. Dr Lindgren kept a busy social calendar and always had someone scuttling round carrying out errands. Strangely enough, Alan seemed to spend longer out on the hill during her visits. I wonder why?

There were several occasions when Alan or I would be required to accompany her on the return journey south. Luckily for Alan, she would allow him to take on the role of chauffeur. Unluckily for me, in her world women chauffeurs in their mid-twenties were unheard of, so I had to sit, terrified, in the passenger seat. Her driving was what one might call erratic and, no doubt because she had grown up at a time when there was far less traffic and far less speed, her perception of what was going on around her left something to be desired. She invariably failed to notice traffic lights and zebra crossings and would never overtake big lorries in case she "upset the lorry driver".

When she started the car her foot would be full down on the accelerator and a high-pitched screeching noise would burst from the engine as she prepared for take-off. A trip south with Dr Lindgren was definitely not for anyone of a nervous disposition. If you were, then the only defence was to pretend to be asleep. The stop-offs at various hotels along the way did, however, help to make up for it. Living it up in a plush, centrally heated building, even if it was only for a night or two, was a far cry from Reindeer House and I was prepared to make the most of it.

Although Dr Lindgren never confided in us and seemed to enjoy the employer–employee relationship, on the couple of occasions when Alan or I defied her in person she certainly took it to heart. Alan was on the whole very loyal to her and she admired him for his hill sense and management of the reindeer. To be fair to her it was very seldom that she denied him anything in pursuit of the wellbeing of the herd. If he needed to order more feed the extra expense was not questioned. Calling in the vet, buying material for mending fences, deciding when and where he should go to find stray reindeer or to gather the herd, all this was very much left to Alan's judgement. On the one occasion when Dr Lindgren did prevent him from doing what he wished, things went horribly wrong and I doubt whether she ever forgot it.

The general routine that Alan had established with the herd was to keep the cows with their newly born calves in the fenced enclosure until the end of May and then to turn them out so that they could range freely and be left, up to a point, to their own devices. Every few days Alan, either on his own or in the company of myself or the current volunteer, would head out on to the hill to check them over.

At the time of one particular calving Dr Lindgren had arranged for a journalist to go on the hill with Alan to see the cows and calves in the enclosure before they were let out on to the free range. The journalist in question had postponed her visit until after the date Alan had intended to put the cows and calves out and there had been a certain amount of discussion between him and Dr Lindgren as to whether they should be held back. Eventually, and very much against his better judgement, Alan gave in and the cows and calves stayed put, awaiting the arrival of the journalist at eleven o'clock on the Monday morning.

At first light Alan was up on the ski road in the van spying through the binoculars to ensure that all was well with the herd. But he quickly detected that all was definitely not: one of the cows, Aina, was running about, calling, obviously searching for her calf. Some hundred yards from her a dog fox was running off with something in his mouth. Alan tore down the hill in the van to the river crossing to get to the enclosure and try to rescue Aina's calf. But the deed was done. The calf was dead in the heather, its head missing. Aina was frantically running around, tricked by the fox and unsure of what had happened to her calf.

Already angry at having to keep the herd back from the safety of the higher ground in the first place, Alan was now furious. He picked up the calf and stormed off the hill to confront Dr Lindgren. It was still very early in the morning. I was just rising and had yet to take her her breakfast. Alan arrived with a squeal of brakes, burst into the house and went straight into Dr Lindgren's room, flinging the headless corpse on the bed. I sat quaking, wondering what all the commotion was about.

Relating the story to me later, Alan said he had no regrets about what he had done because he felt so strongly that the calf's death could so easily have been avoided. In an effort to dissipate his anger, Dr Lindgren asked, "Which fox do you think did it?" No doubt Alan had a suitable reply. Dr Lindgren only mentioned the incident to me once. She said that she had never realised until that day just how committed Alan was to the reindeer. I think her respect for him went up a peg that morning.

When I was expecting our first child Dr Lindgren arranged to be at Reindeer House, which was just about the last thing I needed. She kept asking me what she should do if it all happened sooner than expected, which only made me all the more nervous. How was I to know? When the baby's arrival became imminent I felt that the best place to be was in hospital rather than Reindeer House, with Dr Lindgren and her companion, Mrs Cox, clucking around me.

It was early February and there was a lot of snow. Unable to contact Alan, who was out on the hill working on the opening shot of a film, I decided to call the district nurse, who promptly sent up an ambulance. As I got up into the ambulance I heard Dr Lindgren say to the driver, "You take care of her now – she's a very important person." I felt quite honoured. During the two days I was in hospital she tactfully departed for Cambridge and I returned with young Alex, thankfully, to an empty house.

Motherhood had taken me by storm. I was of course utterly convinced that Alex was the most beautiful baby I had ever seen. The poor postman, the first visitor at the house after I arrived home, was promptly hauled into the sitting room to see the baby sleeping in his cradle. The postman seemed very nervous, scuttling out again as quickly as he could. The next day he was most apologetic. When I had shown Alex to him, he explained, he did not have any "silver" coins in his pocket to leave the baby for good luck. That accounted for his speedy departure.

Dr Lindgren appeared to be completely uninterested in our young son. I certainly cannot ever remember her cooing at him in his cot. She offered no words of wisdom regarding child care, leaving me to get on with it, which suited me fine. On only one occasion did I ask her to babysit. Alex was just over a year old and Alan needed me to help put the cows out of the enclosure after the calving season. That meant being up at first light and possibly not getting back until after Alex had woken up.

A few days beforehand I approached Dr Lindgren to ask if she could keep an eye on him. The thought of being in charge of a young baby obviously weighed heavily on her mind. She asked me over and over again what she should do if he woke up. I told her to lob a few toys in to him. As we were leaving I popped into her room to say we were off and once again she began quizzing me regarding her duties. Since Alex always ate like a horse (and still does) I said, "I know. If he wakes up before I'm down, give him a banana." Dr Lindgren looked taken aback. How was she to feed it to him? "Like a monkey," was my final piece of advice as I headed for the door. Reindeer duties completed, I returned to Reindeer House to find that there was nothing for any of us to worry about. Alex was still sound asleep – which is more than can be said for Dr Lindgren.

The only great sadness in my life has been the death of my mother when Alex was only seven months old. The news came when Dr Lindgren was in residence at Reindeer House and she was very kind, driving me south, with Alex, for the funeral. My mind was too full of sadness to recall the journey. However, I have always remembered her words of wisdom and kindness. "Don't dwell in the past," she said, "your future lies in Alex and Alan." She was absolutely right, of course, and it is advice I have since passed on to others.

She was one of those people whom you somehow imagine will live for ever. For nearly ten years she had been such a dominant factor in our lives that we had no concept of what life at Reindeer House would be like without her. As she grew older there were occasions when I knocked on her bedroom door and there was no answer. I remember thinking to myself on more than one occasion, "Oh my goodness, perhaps she is dead." But she was always fine and the tray with porridge and tea would once again be most welcome.

On the morning she did die, it never crossed my mind when there was no response to my knock. But as soon as I entered the room I knew. There was something in the atmosphere. She looked very peaceful and I turned tail, closing the door behind me. I shook Alan awake and told him, suggesting he went to check, just to make sure. Still half asleep, he could not grasp the enormity of the situation and said he needed time to think first. So I went back to make sure. But there was no mistake. It was March 23, 1988 and she was eighty-three years old. Her family was informed and her son, John, flew up to handle the formalities. Everything happened so quickly: suddenly we were alone in Reindeer House. It was the end of an era.

Ironically, Mr Utsi, who had been so at home with his reindeer out on the hill, had died in Cambridge. Dr Lindgren, who always wanted to die in her beloved Cambridge, had died in Reindeer House. She used to tell me that if she did die in Scotland and it was summer she must not be allowed "to fester" but must be put in cold store immediately and flown to Cambridge. It would have pleased her that the weather was cold that March.

CHAPTER FOUR

Proud Owners of the Herd

fter Dr Lindgren's death, life at Reindeer House went on much as usual for a while, under the management of her son, John, and Mr Utsi's son, Vincent. However, both men lived in the south of England; both had their own careers and family commitments. Being responsible for eighty hungry reindeer hundreds of miles away in the Highlands of Scotland can only have been a liability. We were not surprised when, eight months later, they decided to put the herd up for sale.

I suppose the possibility of our one day owning the reindeer ourselves had always been there, lurking in the back of our minds, though how or when it might happen we had no idea, nor how we might go about raising the necessary cash. But somehow, when the time came, things seemed to fall into place like the pieces in a jigsaw. When word went out on the grapevine that the herd was on the market we were actively encouraged to put in a bid. We had lived and worked with the reindeer for so long that the prospect of being totally responsible for them was not in the least bit daunting. The only really unknown territory was dealing with solicitors and accountants and persuading a bank manager that there was financial gain to be had in herding reindeer.

By good fortune the solicitor whose name I plucked from *Yellow Pages* had been acquainted with Dr Lindgren in the early 1980s and vividly remembered both her love for reindeer and her tremendous personality. She had given him a small reindeer memento which he still possessed. Visiting him was one of the turning points for us. The advice and contacts with which he supplied us were invaluable. When we waffled evasively in answer to his inevitable question, "How are you going to raise the money?" he suggested he should introduce us to a bank manager he knew in Inverness. It was an inspired choice. This bank manager, Mr Culley, had a great love of the hills and was, among other things, a staunch member of the Hedgehog Preservation Trust. He was sympathetic to our cause and saw his way to allowing us to sign the largest cheque we had ever seen.

On August 4, 1989 the Smith family (which by now included Fiona) gathered in his office, ready to become proud owners of Britain's only herd of reindeer. During the previous week the local newspapers had got wind of the imminent purchase and the phone had never stopped ringing. They were intrigued by the "management buy-out". I had stalled them as long as I could, but eventually the *Inverness Courier* decided it could wait no longer and went to press with the story several hours before the final stages of the deal were completed.

As we sat expectantly in Mr Culley's office that August morning, he opened the day's edition of the *Courier* to be confronted with a full-page article about us. "I see the deal has already been clinched in the eyes of the press," he said. Luckily, he had a good sense of humour. "In view of this sort of publicity it would seem that the bank cannot back out now." Having signed on the dotted line, we dashed home to welcome the morning's batch of visitors gathering at Reindeer House for the eleven o'clock trip to the hill. We were like cats with the cream. We were in control, able to make our own decisions, able to make plans for the future of the herd. It was a great feeling. And nothing that has happened since has altered that.

In reality, of course, it was unlikely that anyone else would have been mad enough to take on such a way-out enterprise. Lacking the knowledge we had acquired of reindeer over the years – where they roam, what illness they are susceptible to, what their limitations are – it would have been extremely difficult for an outsider to take over the business with any degree of confidence and learn it all from grass roots.

The herd had never reached the sort of numbers where meat production could become a viable proposition, as Mr Utsi had hoped in the beginning, and very early on it had become obvious that their future, as Britain's only herd of reindeer, lay in their interest to the public. Mr Utsi, great showman that he was, had established the tradition of daily guided visits to the hill. And when he was absent the herder of the day would step into the role. For years it had been Alan and I who had been responsible for the eleven o'clock tours to see the reindeer. And it was along this avenue of public appeal that we decided we must go if we were to make our living by reindeer.

The herd was, in fact, rather like an alternative kind of zoo: it gave people an opportunity to see reindeer in their native habitat. In addition, the layout of Reindeer House made it relatively easy to open the big end room to the public. Accordingly, we turned it into a place for visitors to gather, to learn a bit more about reindeer and, in time, to buy that reindeer memento which would remind them of their visit to the Cairngorm Reindeer Centre.

Right from the start I was determined that it would be a unique reindeer shop, not just another gift outlet. We ordered customised items on reindeer themes and began to sell souvenirs made from polished antler. I remember watching one highly suspicious customer scrutinising the antler brooches for a considerable time. When eventually she chose one, she said, "Well, I suppose this one looks the most natural." You just cannot get away from plastic thoughts these days.

We have made the daily visits to the hill very much a hands-on affair. Because the reindeer have plenty of space and we always greet them with a large bag of food, they are amazingly at ease amongst visitors. From the day they are born the calves become used to the presence of humans and, as the summer progresses, and they see other reindeer feeding from somebody's hand, they gradually become bold enough to follow suit. Greedy mothers tend to produce greedy calves and these will often show their more timid brethren the way.

There are only a few, nervous, reindeer who prefer never to be hand fed but even they will eagerly eat the food we put on the ground. The net effect is that whenever we go out on to the hill looking for them, guiding visitors or simply finding those that have strayed from the herd, they will come to us when we call. It is an ideal situation: they have freedom to roam but we still have daily contact with them.

Within the herd each reindeer is recognisable: facial shape and markings, coat colouring and body shape, behaviour and, at the appropriate time of the year, antler shape all help to give each reindeer its individual characteristics. Mr Utsi, who also regarded reindeer as individuals, began the tradition of giving them names, something which we continue to this day.

Each year we choose a different theme for the calves' names. One year it was birds, another rivers, another Scottish towns; metals, flowers, fish, mountains, moths and butterflies have all given us inspiration. One visitor suggested we used the names of politicians. Thankfully, we have not had to resort to that yet.

I often wonder at what threshold it would become impossible to recognise any more individuals by name. Alan tends to fall into the trap of only seeing the calf as a reflection of its mother but the time comes when you have to give it a name and think of it as a separate reindeer. I know that on the rare occasion when I have been away for a few weeks I sometimes have to rack my brain to put the right name to the right calves when I get back. If I went away for three months I would probably have to re-learn quite a few of them.

The problem is that reindeer are constantly changing in appearance. I make a positive effort to get to know them as calves, but then when they are yearlings they all tend to look the same, all have the same sized bodies and the same sized antlers. Once they are grown up and start having calves of their own or, in the case of the castrated males become Christmas reindeer, they develop their own characters again.

It was because of the reindeer's individuality that we were able to begin the adopt-a-reindeer scheme, which has become a valuable extra source of income towards the upkeep of the herd. To begin with it was all very amateur – I cringe when I look back on the original newsletters I sent out. Luckily, a computer-buff-cum-reindeer-fanatic offered to take over the presentation and nowadays our biannual newsletters are much more professionally produced.

Each year we try to offer supporters something different. We have had photos taken and certificates printed and in the third year I decided to trace the reindeer's family trees. I managed to trace today's herd back to four female reindeer brought in by Mr Utsi, of which Vilda has undoubtedly been the main influence. A fantastic breeder, she produced females who also bred very successfully.

The white strain, too, of which Ferrari is a recent example, traces back to one of the original forest reindeer, Assa. Although Assa was not white herself, most of her calves and descendants have been. White reindeer are definitely the most popular with the public and head the top-ten list of most adopted reindeer. Ferrari, Tiger and Jura currently all have a healthy fan club.

We now have an extremely faithful following of supporters, with an annual re-adoption rate of around 65 per cent. People usually adopt at the time of their visit, though some contact us because they have read about the herd in newspaper or magazine articles. People adopt reindeer for different reasons. Some pick out one they met on the hill, perhaps one that fed out of their hand, one who was particularly friendly or else one who was diffident and needed encouragement. Others are happy just to be assigned a reindeer of our choice.

Some like to choose a reindeer whom nobody else has adopted. One lady who wanted to do this ended up with Hannah, who was already extremely old and died shortly afterwards. When I wrote to break the news she asked to adopt the next oldest. Other reindeer, like Beauty, whom people saw being hand-reared, are very well adopted.

We have always tried to keep it on a friendly basis. People can ring up and ask how "their" reindeer is and we put lots of news about the herd and the weather and their individual reindeer in the newsletters. The only down side is that reindeer do die, and then we have to write and tell people. Some are rather unlucky and keep choosing reindeer who then expire. Sometimes I cannot bring myself to write to people straight away. We have had one or two letters from schools who have joined the scheme to say what a wonderful way it has been of introducing children to death! Generally, though, the feedback is good.

For all this we are still a very modest enterprise. Road signs directing people to the Reindeer Centre probably conjure up images of a theme park on the scale of Alton Towers. Nothing could be further from the truth. On arrival many people, obviously with the wrong idea in their mind's eye, are flustered by the lack of prominent car parking facilities.

One day a rather harassed couple turned up, having followed our Reindeer Centre signs from the main A9 trunk road some ten miles away. They immediately headed round to the paddock to see the reindeer that were down off the hill at the Centre. It was the summer of 1991 and we were hand-rearing Jura. The husband suddenly came storming into the shop and confronted one of our young assistants, Sarah.

"I have just driven fifteen miles off the main road," he told her, "following AA signs for the Reindeer Centre, and all I find when I get here is a poxy shop and a couple of sheep." I wish I had been there. I would have enjoyed asking him to show me the "sheep". As for poor Jura, he must have been mortified to be so described.

One of our biggest steps forward since buying the reindeer has undoubtedly been the establishment of a new base where we now operate a second herd: no longer are the Cairngorms the only area of Scotland where reindeer graze. During the years when we were working for Dr Lindgren we had bought our own house near Tomintoul, thirty miles from Reindeer House. It was an old farmhouse, in need of total renovation and Dr Lindgren was horrified when we took it on. She thought that Alan had quite enough to cope with, with a wife, young children and the reindeer to look after. But for Alan it has been a real labour of love. Up until then he had lived his whole life in places that belonged to someone else; now, at last, he had a home of his own.

As soon as he had a moment's spare time he would be over there, working like a demon, ripping out the inside, putting in insulation, repairing the roof, fitting new doors and windows. Nowadays, while I concentrate on keeping things going at the Reindeer Centre, he tends to spend more of his time at Tomintoul, with the children and me joining him at weekends. The reason for this division of labour is, of course, reindeer.

From our observations during many a winter on the Cairngorms we had noticed that, although the reindeer foraged for lichens, they also spent a lot of time grazing on the newly re-seeded grass at the side of the ski road, as well as on the actual ski area. This made us think that perhaps reindeer do not necessarily rely as totally on lichen as Mr Utsi had led us to believe. From reading about reindeer in other parts of the world, too, it was clear that some, for instance island populations, do not feed on lichens at all.

The terrain around our house at Tomintoul seemed to us to have all the right ingredients for reindeer. If we could gain access to some land there, we could split the herd and so lighten the load on the sparser grazing of Cairngorm where pressures from other users are continually increasing.

We approached the local tenant farmer, Mr McArthur, and asked if he would mind our grazing a few reindeer on his ground. He was pleased to experiment and in January 1990 we selected some of the herd to take across. Unsure whether the reindeer would settle in a new environment, we decided to take very tame Christmas reindeer so that if they did decide to go walkabout we would be able to retrieve them without too much difficulty. We also put big orange collars on their necks with our telephone number, just in case anyone found them straying.

In the event the collars proved unnecessary, for the reindeer were evidently perfectly happy in their new surroundings and never strayed to any serious extent. When they did go slightly out of bounds they always went as a group and it was easy enough to herd them back. Just as we had suspected, they enjoyed the newly re-seeded fields and, because of the good grazing, grew tremendous sets of antlers.

The gentleman's agreement we had with our farmer friend was a great stepping stone for us. It gave us the confidence to pursue the prospect of finding a more permanent site in the vicinity. Through a tip-off from our vet, we discovered that an adjacent hill farm was coming up for let. The site looked ideal for the establishment of a permanent second herd.

I wrote to the Crown Commission, landowners of the Glenlivet Estate, and shortly afterwards received a phone call from their development officer. He said he was most intrigued by our request to establish a herd of reindeer in the Glenlivet area, the more so because, when driving through the estate on the day he received our letter, he had seen reindeer already happily grazing away on the hillside. At this point I thought I had really blown it. I waffled on about it being a small experiment, our only having a few reindeer on the farmer's land, and so on, and hoped for the best.

The Glenlivet Estate is renowned for rearing fine hill sheep and cattle. A herd of reindeer might well appear to go against all the normally accepted rules of stock keeping. What we were looking for was an area with a good mix of heather moorland, grassland and wetland. We knew from bitter experience that reindeer cannot survive on grass alone but require a broad spectrum of browse and grasses and the freedom to move on when they feel the need.

After some months of discussion and negotiation we were delighted when our bid for the tenancy of the farm was successful. On May 31, 1991 we herded our little group of reindeer, who had happily spent the previous year and a half on our neighbour's farm, to the new ground. Mr McArthur and his wife were, I think, rather sad to see them go. They had greatly enjoyed watching them wander across the hillside from their window.

Our new establishment quickly evolved into something more like a ranch than a farm. Fences that had previously kept in stock were opened up to allow the reindeer free access to the land. With a permanent site to play with, we began to syphon off reindeer from the Cairngorm group to make up the numbers at Glenlivet. Most of the reindeer we moved across adapted well, though one or two did wander off at first.

Prince, who had come to us from Chester Zoo, decided to leg it quite soon after we moved him. He, poor lad, lacked any vestige of normal reindeer common sense – presumably because of his zoo upbringing, and who can blame him? He ended up peacefully chewing the cud in someone's prize flower garden. The owner was most concerned about his roses, despite our reassurances that reindeer do not like them. In due course Prince was safely returned to the fold and successfully settled in at the second attempt.

Mackerel, on the other hand, was in a different league. The Cairngorms are clearly visible from our new ranch and when he, who had been born and bred on the mountains, decided to leave Glenlivet, he made a beeline for home, negotiating roads, fences and a river before we caught up with him. We kept hearing reported sightings and Alan spent a whole day searching for him. Then, just as he was about to give up, a friend spotted Mackerel in the middle of a field, tangled up in wire. Having enmeshed his antlers, could stray no further.

As with any land that has been heavily browsed and grazed for many years and repeatedly fertilised and re-seeded, our farm was predominantly grassland, with only small pockets of woodland, which steadily degenerate when there is a high density of stock. In the reindeer's native land there is an abundance of birch woodland and a much richer diversity of plant species. With this in mind, we decided to try, in the long term, to recreate a habitat that included plenty of birch, both mature and regenerating, together with a herb-rich grassland.

One of the problems when allowing regeneration is the thick grassy sward which grows and inhibits tree growth. Professional foresters break up the ground with the latest machinery before planting. But machinery and manpower are expensive and anyway we wanted to adopt a more natural approach. What better, we decided, than the pig?

Anyone who has ever watched a pig at work will hardly have failed to appreciate the strength of his snout. What we needed was a pig that was fairly hardy and did not take too much looking after, so we opted for a small group of Iron Age pigs, wild boar crossed with domestic pigs. They are very hairy and will happily sleep outside.

Because they are driven by an insatiable desire for food, pigs are not the easiest of animals to keep on your side of the fence and it was some time before we found the right environment: a combination of electric fencing, plenty of ground to romp around in and sufficient good food to keep them on home ground. But that very desire for food makes them very effective indeed at turning over turf, which is just what we needed for our tree seedlings.

Unlike the reindeer, we have not given all our pigs names. But we have named the pioneers: Charlie, the big boar; Susie, the light sow; Scoop, the number two boar – though having seen the damage he did to Charlie when they last got together, I have a feeling Scoop might now consider himself number one. The two used to live in tolerable harmony but then we rented Scoop out as a sire for someone else's pigs. When he returned he and Charlie engaged in an awe-inspiring half-hour battle, using their tusks with a slashing action and gouging each other's sides as they whirled round and round. Separating a couple of tons of fighting boar was by no means easy. We succeeded, eventually, but it certainly taught us not to let these two get together ever again.

Seven years from now, people told us, you will be sick and tired of them and never want to keep a pig again. Charlie certainly wasted no time in trying our patience. Our land at Glenlivet is divided into two parcels with some ground in between that is not ours. Charlie and his sows are at Inverchor, and Scoop and his sows at Balcorrach, where our house is.

One day when we were sitting in the kitchen at Balcorrach having a drink I looked outside and to my horror caught sight of Charlie and his sows snorting around the house. He had led them all solemnly across from Inverchor and was now becoming very hot under the collar, having just encountered some young Balcorrach females he had not met before. As we scuttled around, trying to drive him into one of the barns, Alan opened a gate and the pony, Katie, got out. She and Charlie ended up having a bit of a fracas in which she kicked him really hard right on the nose. That pulled even Charlie up in his tracks. He turned away and as he did so we managed to usher him and his ladies into the steading (farm buildings) and shut them all in, later taking them back to their rightful home. He has not been back – yet.

The grand design at Glenlivet is to fence areas off, let the pigs turn the ground over, allow it to regenerate and eventually let the reindeer graze in the resulting birch woodland which is their natural Scandinavian habitat. Less grazing in the fields and more in the woodland, with its different flora under the trees, would be the best for them in the long run. Whether we start a visitors' centre there remains to be seen. Some tourists do come through the area and we are probably well enough known from the Cairngorm Centre for others to make a detour off the beaten track.

One thing is certain. Had we not taken on this new land at Glenlivet, we should certainly have been unable to take advantage of a remarkable gift that, unknown to us at the time, was to come our way.

CHAPTER FIVE

Spring: Calving

The reindeer's life cycle begins in May, nature having sensibly arranged it so that the female reindeer, or cows, have their calves when food is plentiful: the abundance of newly growing leaves, grass and shrubs ensure that mothers and calves thrive.

In the wild, tundra-dwelling reindeer such as the caribou of Alaska are renowned for their lengthy spring migration northwards. In their quest for the best food and to escape harassment from biting insects, they travel thousands of miles, using traditional migration routes, to enjoy the brief Arctic summer. Rivers flooded with melted snow are no impediment, for reindeer are good swimmers, their large hooves serving as paddles and their hollow hair providing great buoyancy.

Woodland reindeer do not undertake such lengthy migrations. There is a seasonal movement out on to the mountains or to the coast in summer to cool off and escape insects, but the distances involved are small in comparison with the tundra-dwellers. Because of their location some reindeer – island inhabitants, for example – cannot migrate because there is nowhere to go. Regardless of the weather conditions they have to stay put and if food becomes scarce, they must rely on their body reserves to tide them over.

For those that do migrate, the instinct to do so is very strong. Fortunately for us, forty-odd years of living on the Cairngorms, with no need to migrate, seems to have blunted the urge among our herd. I do wonder, however, whether Mr Utsi had problems in the early days and whether some of the reindeer which he "lost" were simply following their natural instinct to move to pastures new.

Because in their natural environment the herds would already be on the move during the calving season, reindeer calves are of necessity very precocious. Measuring about eighteen inches high at the shoulder, long-legged and strong, they can stand almost as soon as they are born and within twenty-four hours can keep up with the migrating herd. By the time they are a week old they are already showing a keen interest in grazing and browsing. Feeding on the plentiful plant life helps supplement the milk produced by their mothers. Having weighed in at about ten to fifteen pounds at birth, they may be in excess of sixty to seventy pounds by the end of the summer.

At birth they are normally brown with a dark brown back. Unlike Bambi, reindeer calves do not have spots. At about two months of age the calf coat gives way to the adult coat and by the autumn the calves will have matured into mini-adults, complete with mini-antlers.

Interestingly, whereas wild reindeer (or caribou as they are known in North America) tend to be of the same uniform greyish, brownish colour, in the domesticated herds of Scandinavia there is much more colour variation. Most highly prized of all is white. The Sami people believe that white reindeer are lucky, a tradition which no doubt stems from the fact that shamans, or witch doctors, always wore coats made of white pelts. There is also a belief that more white reindeer occur where there is a preponderance of white rock in the landscape. Hence Mr Utsi's habit of painting stones white on the hills to give nature a helping hand.

Within our Scottish herd about 10 per cent of the reindeer are white and it appears to be a female-generated gene: a white cow will tend to produce white calves, whereas running a white bull through the herd for the season will not necessarily result in normal coloured cows having white progeny. Most people find white reindeer particularly attractive. I like them, too, not only because they are lovely to look at but also because they stick out like sore thumbs, particularly in summer, and so are easy to spot when you are searching for the herd out on the hill. They do, however, tend to be on the small side – in fact the Sami people used to say that white reindeer weren't good survivors. Because of their smaller build, Alan does not like using them as breeding bulls.

One of the main jobs for us in the early spring, before the cows get ready for calving, is the routine worming and vaccinating of all the reindeer, males and females alike. Mr Utsi never wormed the herd, but we find that by dosing them in spring and then a couple of times more during the summer, it makes a lot of difference to their condition. Towards the end of March we herd them into a penned area and give them their injections. Like other ruminants they are susceptible to parasite burdens.

Although our reindeer are used to human company, like most animals they would prefer not to be given injections, and we need a small band of assistants to help worm the herd. Quietly, we lure them into the pen with the help of some tempting food, then drive them into the splendidly sturdy wooden shelter specially built by Alan. Since there is no vehicular access, all the raw materials had to be heaved up the hillside. It was a mammoth task but certainly makes the task of injecting the reindeer easier.

The strongest of our assistants hold each reindeer in turn while Alan adminsters the necessary doses; someone else stands by to hold the syringes, while another is armed with clipboard and pen to note down the name of each animal as it is treated. After ensuring that each reindeer has had the necessary jabs the herd is returned to the hill and we settle back to wait for the cows to start calving, which usually happens from the beginning of May onwards.

Normally reindeer produce just the one calf each year. Mr Utsi used to say that reindeer never have twins, and Dr Lindgren agreed that it had certainly never been proved in the wild. Sometimes it might appear that a cow does have two calves, but this is simply because a calf will go to another cow and steal milk alongside an already suckling calf. Reindeer have four teats and it is not unusual to see three or even four calves at the same milk bar at the same time. The cows' udders are tiny and although the milk is produced in very small quantities – no more than about a cupful a day – it is very rich and nutritious and the calves thrive on it.

How surprised Dr Lindgren would have been to know that shortly after her death one of her cows would, incontrovertibly, produce twins. It is the only time it has ever happened in the herd, and sadly they did not survive. Grayling calved about ten days too early. It was a filthy night. One calf was born dead and the other failed to survive the night.

Unlike the calves of the red and roe deer, who tend to be hidden away when they are small, reindeer calves stay with their mothers at all times. In the wild, if they are to survive, this is essential. Not only would they be on migration, but they would also need to be constantly on the watch for bears and wolverine.

I used to think that reindeer made bad mothers because whenever there was a problem they would always run. I felt so sorry for the little calf as it lolloped over the heather trying to keep up. One would think their strategy would be to wait and try to take the calf with them. But of course if you waited for the calf and tried to stand your ground against a large predator you would probably lose not only your calf but your own life as well – and that would be bad policy for the survival of the herd. In the light of this knowledge I reviewed my opinion of reindeer mothers. Reindeer certainly do care about their calves, constantly calling to them with low grunting noises, which the calves answer in the same tone of voice.

Over the years, Alan has taken full responsibility for the calving season of our herd, getting up at first light, walking out to find any separated reindeer, checking on the strength of the calf and gently moving the pair back to smaller fenced areas so that he can keep an eye on them. People often ask us why there are not more reindeer in this country. The answer is simple: keeping reindeer in their natural habitat involves too much work for most people. Sometimes in the spring the herd will be three-quarters of an hour's walk away, or you might spend all day looking for a cow that has gone missing and might have calved and still not find her.

These days everyone who farms wants to bring their animals inside, not trek out to the hills to tend them, which is hardly cost effective! With reindeer you just cannot do that. You have to commit yourself to a lot of time plodding around. So many people imagine that we reach the herd by four-wheel-drive vehicle. They are appalled when we say we have to use Shanks's pony. Reindeer need to be on the hills, on open heather moorland with the lichens, mosses and sedges that they are designed to eat.

Because they live in such a relatively wild habitat there will, inevitably, be losses through natural causes. With no wolves to bother them in Scotland, the main dangers for our newly born calves are falling into deep water holes, or being attacked by the red fox. Naturally, Alan takes every possible precaution, but if he tried to fence every deep hole on the hillside he would still be doing it now, so there is always an element of chance.

Snowdrop, one of our white reindeer, lost her calf down

a water hole in circumstances that gave the calf no chance whatever. The silly old thing had actually calved straight into the hole, so the poor calf never even managed to raise its head. It was such a shame. It was a beautiful slate grey calf with a white star on its forehead. It was a good size, too, and would have been totally healthy. Poor Snowdrop was distraught. All her feelings were centred on tending a calf, she had bags of milk, and all she could do was look longingly at all the other youngsters running around with their mothers.

My own first experience of finding a drowned calf was equally frustrating. Trout calved at first light. Alan had been across to her, checked out a strong bull calf, and left the pair of them, with Trout licking the calf's coat dry. At eleven o'clock I went on to the hill with some visitors and our daughter, Fiona, who was four and a half at the time. After showing the visitors the herd, Fiona and I headed off further into the hills to check on Trout and her newly born. The awful sight that met our eyes was Trout's calf lying limp and lifeless in a pool of water, with Trout gazing down at him helplessly.

Too late to be of assistance, I pulled the little body out and left Trout to lick him dry. After seeing my look of despair, Fiona commented, "Don't worry, Mummy, Trout will have another calf next year." She was right, of course, and her little voice helped put the day's events into perspective. Later, when Trout had become accustomed to her loss, Alan went out and collected the dead calf.

Occasionally, too, the vet has to be called to perform a Caesarian operation. When she was a four-year-old, a cow called Stream was taking so long to calve that Alan sent for Mr Rafferty as we could not tell whether it was a breech birth or whether she was just too weak to produce the calf herself. By the time the vet arrived poor Stream could hardly walk. The stress of trying to calve was weakening her every minute so Mr Rafferty decided to perform the Caesarian there and then on the hillside.

Thousands of years of domestication and, in recent times, daily contact with both us and scores of visitors, have resulted in our reindeer being pretty amenable to being handled and restrained. Accordingly, Alan was able to hold Stream without causing her undue stress while the vet injected her with a sedative. After a few minutes her legs buckled underneath her and he lowered her gently down on to her side.

Fiona was there, her eyes popping out on stalks as Mr Rafferty made the first incision. Stream's calf was a fairly big male, lying rather awkwardly and looking pretty lifeless when the vet hauled him out. Having cleared the mucus from his nose and mouth, Mr Rafferty held on to his back legs and swung him round his head, a method that apparently improves circulation. By this stage I was convinced that Fiona was going to grow up with a very strange view of childbirth. While Mr Rafferty began to sew Stream back up again, Fiona and I rubbed the calf dry, his mother being too doped to care.

Although mother and calf survived, the operation had left Stream with no maternal instincts whatever for her new-born and we had to resort to hand-rearing the wee chap. It is never easy to hand rear any young animal straight from birth. It is imperative that they suckle the mother's colostrum, the first milk, which is rich in important antibodies to protect the youngster against disease. In desperation we ended up driving to a local dairy farm to get some cow's colostrum. Sadly, after ten days, we lost him. But at least Stream was all right. Since then she has successfully produced five fine calves, Talisker, Cashew, Skipper, Crag and, most recently, Saturn.

To digress for a moment, speaking of Mr Rafferty reminds me of an amusing incident one day when he had been examining a reindeer in the paddock at the house. Having starred in the BBC TV series *The Vet* Mr Rafferty strikes a familiar chord with many of our visitors. On this particular day he had spent some time examining the sick reindeer and as we left the reindeer paddock a middle-aged woman came scuttling up to him and said, "Are you Mr Rafferty from the tele?" Mr Rafferty replied that he was, whereupon our visitor said, "Would you mind if I touched you?" I was so embarrassed, but Mr Rafferty did not bat an eyelid.

"By all means, Madam," he replied, and the woman went away quite content, having come into contact with a real-life television star.

During the spring the reindeer's appearance begins to change. If they have not already lost them during fights over food in the winter, the cows will cast their antlers around calving time. The bulls meanwhile, having been antlerless during the winter, are now sporting considerable new growth. Even the calves, at a few weeks old, will start to produce bumps on their heads in readiness for their first set of antlers. All in all it is a wonderful time of growth and regeneration – my favourite season of the reindeer year.

CHAPTER SIX

Summer Hazards

As the days lengthen into summer the reindeer shed their winter coats. During June they look so amazingly scruffy and moth-eaten that we seem to spend most of our time apologising to visitors for their distinctly shabby appearance. I often wonder what people think when friends produce their holiday photos of their trip to Scotland and their visit to the Reindeer Centre at this time of year.

Normally the coat begins to moult first from around the eyes, leaving dark rings that make the eyes look even bigger than they already are. Then, as the light-coloured winter hair starts to fall out by the handful, the short, dark summer coat is gradually revealed. I once made the mistake of suggesting to a school party on the hill that they could speed up the process of moulting and make the reindeer more elegant by pulling the loose winter coat out. While we stood there, a greedy old bull called Oak was eating out of the feedbag, oblivious of the school children all huddled around him. I suddenly realised to my horror that they weren't just pulling out loose hair but were literally plucking him alive. His winter coat wasn't really ready to moult and, as they removed his hair, there was nothing growing underneath. To avoid ending up with a bald reindeer, plucking was halted. I never suggested the idea again to a potentially over-zealous school party.

Reindeer hair is too short to be used for spinning, although it can be spun when mixed with wool. Indeed, in the early 1960s it was turned into a fashionable type of cloth. In years gone by the hair was also used for stuffing upholstery, but that practice has long since been superseded by man-made fibres.

As the reindeer's summer coats come through towards the end of July the whole herd begins to take on a wonderfully sleek appearance, enhanced by the velvet antlers, which grow so rapidly that you can virtually see the difference on a daily basis. We handle the reindeer as little as possible at this time of year, to avoid damaging the soft antlers.

There was one summer when some of the reindeer's coats did not look quite as glamorous as usual. We had heard of a wonderful new wormer which did not have to be injected but could be poured on the reindeer's backs. People use it for cattle and it is simply absorbed through the skin. It seemed such a good idea and so much less stressful than giving injections. There was just one problem: two days later the reindeer's hair fell out. When we rang the vet to find out what was going on he said he had meant to warn us: apparently cattle people never use it on their pedigree show cows for the same reason.

Our problem, of course, was the Christmas reindeer. What were they going to look like later in the year? The hair did re-grow, but it came through as their early winter coat, so they ended up with a light stripe along their backs – and a none too straight a line either, since the reindeer had evidently been moving about while I was pouring the wormer on. Ah well, you learn from experience.

Throughout the summer months the reindeer loll around on the high tops, seeking out snow beds to lie on and cool mountain breezes to keep the flies away. If the air is very thick and humid and the flies really troublesome, the reindeer huddle together – perhaps in the vain hope of passing their quota on to their next-door neighbour. Compared with their relatives across the North Sea, though, our reindeer have a relatively easy time. In Scotland the biting insects are mainly restricted to midges, which do not seem to bother the reindeer unduly. In northern Scandinavia they have to endure mosquitoes, black fly and sand fly, all of which both bite severely and drive the reindeer crazy with their high-pitched buzzing noises. The typical stance of a reindeer tormented by heat and flies is one of utter dejection. With head hung low and the occasional sharp twitch or stamp of the foot, they must long for the cold days of winter.

One theory for reindeer growing antlers is that it enables them to radiate heat in the summer. It can certainly be a difficult season for them. At the very time when they should be putting on weight, ready for the rut and the bleak winter months, and when they have access to plentiful food, they inevitably spend long periods not eating but lying on snow patches trying to keep cool. It can be particularly hard on the calves if the cows will not get up for them to suckle.

Whereas in the tundra regions old reindeer tend to die in the winter when they are unable to break through the ice to reach food, we find our old reindeer are more likely to die in summer. Dr Lindgren wrote that in Manchuria, the most southerly part of the reindeer's range, the old animals always die in summer, too, not in winter.

Even fit, healthy reindeer are not entirely free from danger out on the hill in the summer months, as we have found to our cost. There is no doubt that reindeer are capable of being quite clumsy. They are certainly not as agile as sheep or goats and will avoid steep slopes or boulder-strewn areas if they can. Twice Alan has stumbled upon reindeer who have obviously died as a result of falling.

Once, while he was gathering a small group together, the reindeer jumped a burn some 200 yards ahead of him.

As he came down to jump it himself something caught his eye. Looking down he could see a reindeer cow lying in the stream, stone dead. She was still warm and had obviously slipped going over the stream, fallen and broken her neck.

A similar accident must have befallen a three-month-old calf called Cobalt, though she was luckier. Alan found her hobbling along with a broken leg – presumably she had slipped and fallen awkwardly, perhaps after being shoved by another reindeer. Her foreleg was broken high up near the shoulder. Because trying to carry her with a broken leg would only have made things worse, Alan walked her gently back to the enclosures with the rest of the herd. Mr Rafferty was called and fitted her with the sort of high-tech, lightweight plaster cast used on racehorses.

Cobalt and her mother Cam spent the rest of the summer in a small pen, getting lots of food which resulted in Cam growing the most wonderful set of antlers – possibly the best I have ever seen. After a few weeks Mr Rafferty removed Cobalt's plaster. The leg had mended successfully enough, but unfortunately it no longer bent at the joint. Giving a reindeer physiotherpy would have been somewhat problematical, so Cobalt had to survive on the hill with a stiff leg. Although she moved awkwardly, swinging her leg out to the side, she managed admirably, keeping up with the herd and even managing to calve successfully. We were so proud of her that day, though sadly her calf did not survive.

As the years went by, however, she found it more and more difficult to get across the hillsides and could not keep up with the herd. Normally reindeer's feet need no attention because they wear down naturally as they move about on the hills. But because Cobalt could not walk properly on her stiff leg, her hoof did not wear down and needed regular clipping. Reindeer that we have bought from zoos tend to have the same problem but their over-long feet wear down naturally once they start roaming around on the hills in search of food.

In the case of Cobalt, we eventually decided that the kindest thing was to give her an easier life by finding her a home in captivity, where she did not have to work quite so hard to find food. We knew of a lady who wanted to buy a reindeer, so we let Cobalt go. She lived to a ripe old age and at the end of the day I do believe that mending her leg, rather than putting her down, had been the right thing to do.

Cam's spectacular antlers are in the exhibition room at Rendeer House as a fitting memorial to them both. When we returned the pair to the hill I kept hoping that I would be there when Cam shed them. But of course it never happens like that. We even considered the possibility of tying a string on to her antlers and fastening it around her neck so that when they did fall off they would remain attached. One day she came over the hill with the herd and they were gone. Alan made a mental note of the direction she had come from and six months later came across them while out walking. They were unmistakably Cam's and I was delighted when he turned up with them.

Except when they have been involved in an accident, like Cobalt, reindeer are seldom lame. Sometimes as they become older they might become a little arthritic, but the stiffness tends to come and go and does not usually become too serious.

The distinctive clicking noise that reindeer make when they walk has nothing to do with arthritis or any other problem for that matter. It is produced by a tendon, situated across the lower joint in the leg. It always reminds me, rather painfully, of a dodgy knee, but for the reindeer it has great advantages.

For animals with a strong herding instinct it is imperative that all members of the herd stay together because of the danger of attack by large predators such as wolves. The constant clicking of their legs enables the reindeer to keep tabs on each other and prevent them getting lost. As they move along grazing, heads down, the noise acts as a constant reminder of where they are. When a large herd is on the move the clicking sound is tremendous.

Apart from the natural hazards encountered living out on the hills, reindeer face one or two man-made problems, too. In summer, particularly, the hills are popular with walkers and wherever human beings walk they manage to leave a trail of litter in their wake. They also have dogs, and dogs remind reindeer of one thing – wolves.

The litter problem seems to be endless, and it is not just a question of aesthetics. Reindeer can die slow, agonising deaths because of a moment's thoughtlessness on the part of a walker out on the hill. Reindeer are terrors for picking up plastic, polystyrene, tin cans and other rubbish. All too often such items will become stuck in their throats or, if swallowed, cause an obstruction in their intestines. A reindeer that is poorly cannot keep up with the herd and, if it is not discovered by us in time, will just go off and slowly starve to death. One of the reasons why we wanted to move part of the herd from the Cairngorms to Glenlivet was to reduce the number of losses on the hill caused by this very problem.

One year, towards the end of the summer, I offered to go out with the local warden from the Royal Society for the Protection of Birds, who own the next-door estate, to help him with his litter collection. I took along a lovely old reindeer called Bynack, with the intention of packing the litter in panniers on his back. Together we plodded out to the RSPB's bothy, and I was absolutely appalled by the amount of litter we found there. We filled ten plastic bags, far too much for Bynack to carry. We struggled down, each with a load, but about three miles from home I could see that Bynack had had enough. He was so fed up I turned him loose and watched him as he headed off, with evident relief, up the hill. Later we went back to collect the bags.

People mistakenly think Scotland is such a clean place. We never see any litter, visitors say. But the litter is there all right – they just cannot see it. It is often windy on the hills, so as soon as it is dropped it blows straight into the heather, where it lies in wait for unsuspecting animals. Personally, I believe that litter bins simply add to the problem. People toss litter at a bin from yards away and miss, or the wind simply blows it out and disperses it. I prefer people to hold on to their rubbish and take it home with them. That way it cannot do any harm.

As for dogs, they are a perennial problem, too. Or rather some dog-owners are. I well remember the occasion when Rosie and Henry Humphries had come up to prepare for their first Christmas events. We had all gone up on to the hill to fetch the Christmas reindeer to do a mini-event in Aviemore to show Rosie and Henry the ropes. We caught our reindeer and began to lead them down off the hill and through the enclosure gates. The enclosures are near the top of a river bank and just as I was approaching the brow of the bank up came a loose dog. It took one look at the reindeer and started barkly wildly, snapping at Gustav's feet. The only possible way of holding on to a reindeer as strong as Gustav is to sit down, so I plonked myself on the ground.

Poor Alex, leading more reindeer behind me, was less lucky. He was caught totally unawares and his reindeer just pulled away and shot off up the hill. Fiona, who was still close to the fence, had the presence of mind to grab hold of it with one hand, while hanging on to Milligan's lead rope with the other. As she stood there, having her little arms stretched in different directions but resolutely refusing to let her reindeer go, Alan tore down the hill and gave the owners a real piece of his mind. They had just passed a sign saying "Beware reindeer – please keep your dog on a lead" yet were totally oblivious of the chaos they had caused.

In Mr Utsi's time there were certainly instances of loose dogs chasing reindeer into fences or causing cows to abort, the same things that would worry a shepherd with his sheep. Dogs will not kill reindeer but they will upset and disperse them. For this reason we will not let visitors bring their dogs with them. We ask them either to leave them in their cars, or else let them take them so far on to the hill and them tie them to the fence or else keep back away from the herd.

I well remember one day when a visitor insisted on taking his French hunting poodle on to the hill, explaining plaintively that otherwise it would demolish the interior of his car in his absence. As soon as the reindeer saw us they disappeared. They had probably been chased the day before and were not going to stay around to let it happen again. The rest of the visitors looked askance as the reindeer headed up the hillside. They eventually came to a halt and the party struggled up the hill through deep heather to reach them. Needless to say, the man with the poodle turned back.

Although Mr Utsi would never have contemplated having a working dog with him around the reindeer, Alan, on the other hand, has always felt that there was room for a good dog in certain circumstances. When Alex was a baby and I had less time to help with the herd, Alan acquired a young sheepdog, Nelly. She came from a loving owner in the middle of Bradford, complete with a squeaky pink elephant and a note which read, "The pink elephant is her favourite toy. She is a very fussy eater and has to have all her meat chopped up very finely."

Within a week of being with Alan on the hill Nell had put such things behind her and was turning into a wonderful working dog. With one exception the reindeer would never tolerate any dog getting too close, particularly when Alan was in amongst them, feeding them and checking them over, so it was important for Nell not to be too near by. Very quickly she learnt to keep well back: if Alan told her to lie down she did so and would not move until he told her.

The one reindeer who had no fear whatever of Nell was Wally. Hand-reared by Alan, he had been raised in and around the house and was quite used to dogs. If one approached him, he would whap it on the head with his front hoof. Poor Nell got many a bash from him and in the end would turn away and not risk facing him.

Wally was one of the worst offenders for hanging around the ski car park looking for tit-bits from visitors. One of the main reasons for getting a dog in the first place was to cure greedy individuals like Wally of this reprehensible and dangerous habit. On the whole it worked. But not with Wally. While the rest of the herd would hot-foot it up the hill as soon as Nell appeared, Wally would just stand there looking at her.

One day we tried to teach him a lesson. Some friends came to stay, together with their lurcher, Slick. Slick was quite young and very playful and he soon had Wally gambolling across the hill, tail up, as fast as he could go. There was no way that Wally could outrun Slick and, having conceded defeat, he was not seen for the next three days. But even that did not stop him from "car-parking" and he was soon back to his old tricks.

Wally apart, Nell was a wonderful assistant for Alan, quickly becoming his right-hand woman. As he led the reindeer down off the hill, she would chivvy them along from behind. Never getting closer than fifty yards, she would nevertheless keep the herd moving along. At first she relied on his commands to tell her when to move, but before long she was anticipating what to do next, when to come closer or run out to the side to bring a wayward reindeer in. In time it became almost a game of cat and mouse: the reindeer knew Nell and vice-versa.

Unusually for a working dog, Nell was not a one-man dog but would work for me just as well as for Alan, provided we were not both trying to give her orders at the same time, which only confused her. She always went on the hill with the visitors and always stayed back while Alan or I took them to see the herd. If anyone tried to speak to her or stroke her as they walked past, she would studiously ignore them, so intent was she on doing her job.

One day I was out with a couple of visitors and, as usual, Nell was lying well back while we went to see the herd. The couple remarked on how obedient she was and I told them proudly that she would never budge from where I had left her, even if she had to stay there all day. When we got back I wanted the earth to swallow me up. Nell had gone. I could not imagine what had happened.

Scanning the area for any sign of her, I spotted a large group of people walking away into the hill and I wondered if for any strange reason she had decided to follow them. Jumping into the van I drove further up the hill to take a better look at the hill walkers. Sure enough, through my binoculars I could see a black and white dog running along beside the group.

They had a headstart of a good three-quarters of an hour and when I eventually caught up with them, fit though I was, I was absolutely exhausted. And to add to my problems I found that the black and white dog was in fact a springer spaniel. Exasperated, I asked one of the members of the group if they had by any chance seen a black and white collie at the top of the bank near the beginning of their walk.

"Oh yes," someone said, "we found a collie lying near the path but she couldn't move, so two of our party carried her back to their vehicle and were going to take her to the police station in Aviemore."

I was so cross that I was almost speechless. However, I did manage to explain that Nell was not injured but had been told to stay and, being such an obedient dog, would not move until I went back and changed the command.

"But aren't you pleased to know that she is in safe hands?" they asked.

"No!" I replied, just furious that they had made me run across a hillside in pursuit of my dog who had nothing wrong with her but was now sitting in a police station in Aviemore. With that I stormed off back to Reindeer House and rang the police. Two lads had come in with her, they told me, but she was injured and could not move, so they had kindly taken her to the vet in Grantown-on-Spey, fifteen miles away. When I rang Mr Rafferty he, of course, confirmed that there was nothing wrong with the dog, so he had left her at his local police station.

By the time I caught up with her there she had finally given up "doing her job" and was gleefully playing with a well-chewed sock behind the desk. She looked decidedly guilty when she heard our voices. What must she have thought when the walkers picked her up and carried her the half mile off the hill to their vehicle? All the way to the vet she had stayed immobile. Mr Rafferty later recalled that her "rescuers" had blocked his drive as they tried with the utmost difficulty to prise her out of the car. Nell's only failing, it seems, was her inability to talk.

Whereas Nell would certainly never have wandered

off of her own accord with a party of walkers, reindeer often do, much to the amusement of their adopted humans. I had a call at Reindeer House one morning from some people who had been walking all the previous day with Bynack in tow. He had latched on to them shortly after they passed the enclosures. When they met another party of walkers and stopped to talk, Bynack stopped, too. When they carried on, he went rushing after them. They took pictures of each other standing with their arms around him, and of him looking into their rucksack, ever hopeful of finding some food. They had not encouraged him, however, he had simply elected to go for a walk with them. When they eventually got back to their car and drove off, he stood watching them go.

For herding animals it is, as a rule, an advantage to stay together but quite often the bulls like to spend the summer on their own and this is usually when walkers come across solitary ones, who then decide to tag along for company. As the rutting season approaches, however, the bulls begin to rejoin the herd. In August they start cleaning the velvet from their antlers in readiness for the most important part of their year.

CHAPTER 7

Autumn: Out of Velvet, Into Action

The cleaning of the velvet from the antlers heralds the rutting season. The bulls are the first to clean off their velvet, during late August and early September. The cows and calves follow suit in mid-to late September.

This is the month when the bulls fight to establish supremacy, the dominant individuals securing the harems of cows. Their dark summer coats, which last for only about six weeks, are already being replaced by their light-coloured winter ones, which come through first on their necks. Rolling in fat and with their full sets of antlers and contrasting colours, the reindeer really look their best in the autumn.

Most people are fascinated by reindeer antlers and certainly a mature bull with a full set is an incredibly impressive sight. Yet when they first arrive at Reindeer House very few of our visitors have any idea of the remarkable process involved each year in the growing and shedding of these amazing appendages. Hence the not infrequently asked question, "Are their antlers made of wood?"

Antlers are in fact bone and are grown and cast on an annual basis. They are not just for decoration, either, but are of enormous significance to the animals. For the male reindeer antlers are an essential weapon. Fiercely possessive of his harem of females, he uses them to fight off any challengers to his supremacy. The bull reindeer's approach to fighting is more gentlemanly than some other species, though. Reindeer do not generally fight to inflict injury: combat for them is a trial of strength and involves considerable showing off. Their large, complex antlers are used for locking heads for a pushing match. The sparring pair will test each other's strength until one gives way. There is no redress and the loser of the fight will not challenge his rival again.

Unfortunately, reindeer are terrors for getting themselves tangled up not just with each other but also in wire. Fighting on wire fences is a favourite pastime of bulls getting ready for the rutting season, so much so that when I first arrived at Reindeer House it was customary to saw off all the bulls' antlers before the rut began. I well remember one year finding our two main bulls, Trix and Eros, down at the bottom of the enclosure with their antlers firmly encased in the same ball of thick-gauge Forestry Commission wire, which was attached to a telegraph pole. We had to fetch a pair of wire cutters and even then it was a difficult job to free them. The main problem was trying to untangle both at the same time. If one had been freed before the other he would simply have attacked us instead.

The first week in September was the traditional time for lassoing the bulls. Bringing a reindeer bull to the ground is an art in itself. It is a question of technique rather than brute strength, although long arms certainly help. While the lassoer holds on tightly to the antlers, pushing the nose of the reindeer to the ground, the assistant leans over the bull's shoulders, pulls the furthest front leg up from under the animal and brings him down, simultaneously sitting on his shoulder to keep him there. Once he is in this position the antlers can be sawn off. It all sounds so easy – in practice I have been known to set off on an unexpected reindeer ride. In recent years we keep fewer breeding bulls, and we find that there is less fighting and correspondingly less tangling up in fences, so we have not needed to remove their antlers.

One particular autumn stands out in my memory from the days when used to saw off the antlers. I was expecting Fiona at the time, but nothing was going to prevent me from missing the annual ritual. Although I did not actually grapple reindeer to the ground, I did make the walk across to the herd and was kept busy holding back Alex, who was eighteen months old at the time and keen to assist in the operations.

The excitement of the day must have brought me on, because early the next morning Fiona was wanting to make a slightly premature entrance into the world. Alan drove me the thirty-odd miles to hospital, leaving me while he took young Alex to stay with his mother. By the time he returned, things were beginning to happen. It was lunchtime and the midwife must have been feeling a bit peckish because she suddenly headed out of the door. Needless to say, only moments afterwards Fiona decided to pop her head out.

With all the experience he has had in this area, I would have been quite happy for Alan to deliver our children, and in this case he very nearly did. Taking charge with great aplomb, he cupped Fiona's head in his not very pristine hand, at the same time trying to reach the alarm button at the other end of the bed. The midwife was like a clucking hen when she came back.

Deer are the only animals to grow antlers, and the reindeer is unique in that it is not just the bulls who grow them but also the females. The theory is that female reindeer grow them in order to compete successfully for food during the harsh winter months. This makes good sense on two counts: adequate food is particularly important for the pregnant cows if they are to produce fine, healthy calves the following spring and, genetically speaking, it is in the main breeding bull's interest that he does not compete for food with the female who is carrying his calf.

Whether or not the theory is correct, it certainly seems to work that way, since the big bulls are the first to cast their antlers, in the early part of the winter, followed by the young bulls, while the females (unless they happen to break them in fights) keep theirs until the calving season in May. This gives the females the upper hand during the worst of the winter, when food is most scarce. While on the subject of nourishment, very often when reindeer cast their antlers the first thing they do is to eat them – or rather suck them – presumably to get the calcium back into their systems. In fact, some cows are so keen that they suck their calves' antlers while they are still on their heads.

It is fascinating to see the dramatic switch in the supremacy stakes when the main breeding bull loses his antlers. You would think that experience would teach these bulls not to be such bullies when they are antlered. But our most recent one, Crackle, shows no signs of acquiring wisdom with age. During the second half of the year his combination of large body and antlers means that his authority is never challenged. Nobody moves him off his food; when he walks through the herd other reindeer turn away rather than risk a confrontation. He really thinks he is the bee's knees. But when he casts his antlers he gets his come-uppance in no uncertain terms. Usually a reindeer's two antlers cast almost simultaneously, so the transformation is virtually instantaneous.

I was actually with the herd on the hill last winter when Crackle cast his. As I watched, I saw that his loss was immediately spotted by one of the calves, Ayla. Standing only a quarter of his size, she nevertheless had no hesitation in walking straight up to him and challenging him with her little single spikes, no more than three inches long. The humiliation was too much for Crackle. He turned away and walked off, looking extremely dejected. But Ayla had not finished with him. Seeing him walk away when challenged was clearly a source of great enjoyment to her and she continued to pursue him until, presumably, she was satisfied that she had taught him a lesson – and paid him back for all those times when he had given her no mercy. Watching him hanging forlornly around the edge of the herd, trying not to be noticed, it is tempting to feel sorry for him, until you remember how badly he behaves to the others when he has his antlers on.

During the winter months the cows move rapidly up the peck order as first the breeding bulls then the younger ones cast their antlers. Enjoying their new position in the social order, the cows will use their antlers to great effect against the bulls. If you have just dug a hole in the snow to reach food, short spiky antlers are an ideal weapon with which to defend your patch and prevent a bigger, male reindeer from moving you on.

The bossiest reindeer I have ever come across is a cow named Torrent. A very greedy individual, she has two pet hates: young bull reindeer and other young females, like herself, who try to vie for extra food. Her tactics are either to put her head down and chase or, alternatively, to administer a "Glasgow kiss" with a difference. As she brings her head sharply down, a pair of spiky antlers make contact with some poor unsuspecting rival's rump and it is time for him (or her) to move on.

Female reindeer also engage in the same head-to-head combat favoured by males during the rut, though never for long, and the outcome is never cut and dried, as it is in the case of the bulls. Over-zealous females who constantly pick fights invariably break off their antlers before they are due to cast them in the spring, so that as the winter progresses more and more reindeer become antlerless, whether or not they are carrying a calf.

Reindeer start to grow their antlers at a very early age. At three weeks little bumps appear on the calves' heads.

Over the summer these bumps elongate and become furry, just like those of the adults, until by the end of the summer the calves have perfect miniature antlers. Females grow quite big pointed antlers, while the big bulls have massive ones. For bull reindeer, the size of their antlers is relative to age – the older they are the bigger their antlers grow. But, contrary to popular belief, a new point is not added each year. In fact, the shape and complexity of antlers depends on each individual reindeer. Quality of grazing certainly plays a very important role, particularly with the females and calves: the better the grazing, the bigger the antlers. Red deer are a good example of this. A red deer living in the rather impoverished habitat of the Scottish Highlands will grow much less impressive antlers than a red deer living in the comfort of an English deer park.

Like any growing limb, a growing antler needs a supply of blood. Unlike horn, which is composed of a protein called keratin and which grows from the bottom (as in fingernails), antlers grow from the tips. To facilitate this growth, blood is conveyed up through the velvety skin on the outside of the bony part, which is calcifying all the time. During this process the antlers radiate heat, because the blood is so close to the surface. These velvet antlers, as they are known, are soft and sensitive to the touch and during the growing period reindeer are extremely careful not to damage them. Once the antlers are complete, the blood supply is cut off and the velvet skin peels away to reveal solid bone underneath. It is at this stage that the antlers are ready for action.

Antler is the fastest growing living tissue in the animal kingdom and reindeer expend a tremendous amount of energy growing their antlers. For the bulls, particularly, it is a tough time. First they use energy to grow their antlers, then at the height of the rut, when they are busy fighting other bulls and keeping their cows together, they have no time to eat. As a result they often go through the winter badly, looking very thin. Not surprisingly, in the wild at any rate, the winter is usually the time when older bulls die.

For some reason there are reindeer who never grow antlers at all, or only grow one. Personally, I believe it is due to some sort of nutritional deficiency at the crucial time when the calf should have been growing antlers for the first time – at about three weeks. Perhaps the grazing is poor, or the mother's milk has dried up. The weather may have been bad, or the calf is sickly. Certainly, if the antlers do not grow in that first year they never grow. And it is the same with reindeer who grow only one antler – they never grow antlers on the other side. This deficiency does not seem to be inherited. Ferrari, for example, is antlerless, yet she comes from a mother with antlers and produces calves with antlers.

Interestingly, among red deer it is not uncommon to find stags who never grow antlers. They are called hummels and some succeed in holding harems of females against stags with antlers by the simple virtue of their size. Presumably, when you do not grow antlers all the energy that would have gone into those appendages on your head goes instead into your body. To some extent the same applies to reindeer. You would think that not having antlers would be a huge disadvantage, but those who have never had them are by no means at the bottom of the peck order. When reindeer lose their antlers they use their front feet for fighting. Antlerless reindeer do the same – they go straight up on their back legs and strike out with their front feet. These make good weapons. They are sharp and can take chunks of hair out of another reindeer.

As far as humans are concerned, the most important thing when coming into contact with reindeer is never to act like a rutting bull. I explained this one day to a large American tourist out on the hill. Our main bull at the time was Gustav who, unlike most rutting bulls, was quite tolerant of parties of visitors – so long as they did not antagonise him. He was, and still is, a real gentleman among reindeer. Secure in the knowledge that he was dominant, he did not need to waste time entangling his antlers in fences to prove it and consequently we never needed to saw his antlers off.

On this particular day the reindeer and the party of visitors were walking together to a suitable spot for feeding. Gustav was very active, running around to make sure he was not losing any of his ladies. On one of his sorties past the visitors the American suddenly decided, for some reason best known to himself, to start running alongside Gustav. Instantly interpreting this behaviour as a challenge, the normally imperturbable Gustav swung round and flattened the intruder with his antlers. Nobody said anything and the visitor in question was suitably sheepish. I breathed a sigh of relief, safe in the knowledge that only minutes earlier I had explained the potential danger.

CHAPTER EIGHT

Winter:
A Perfectly
Designed Product

F rom the tips of their noses to the soles of their feet, reindeer are perfectly adapted to life in the most inhospitable of climates. Short, round and dumpy in build, their low surface area to body ratio ensures minimum heat loss. The reserves of fat which they lay down during the summer months help combat starvation periods during the Arctic winter, when ice can make it impossible even for reindeer to dig, while their tremendously dense coats are proof against the fiercest blizzard.

As for their feet, there is no better design of "snow shoe" in the world. Significantly, their North American cousins, caribou, take their name from the Micmac Indians' word "Xalibu", meaning digger or scraper. It is the reindeer's capacity to hunt for food with its feet through the deepest of snow that enables it to eke out a living in conditions that few creatures can survive. Reindeer are often described as ungainly and caricatured as clumsy and awkward; but it is their accentuated features that enable them to survive in conditions of incredible severity. Their very large, splayed hooves spread their weight so that they can walk easily on the softest of snow.

Although our Scottish herd live in comparatively mild conditions and never have to dig too far, reindeer living above the Arctic Circle in Russia spend much of the winter in unbelievably harsh conditions. Yet, thanks to their perfectly adapted feet, they can still find enough to eat. I think it is probably true to say that reindeer never dig in vain: they can smell their favourite winter food, lichen, under three feet of snow.

Lichen is found in abundance in the Arctic and sub-Arctic regions and forms the staple diet of most mainland reindeer and caribou in the winter months. One of the main reasons why Mr Utsi chose the Cairngorm area for his reindeer was the rich supply of ground lichen.

Reindeer also have wonderful insulation against the worst that nature can throw at them. They are hairy virtually from nose to toe and the hair is very dense. The hair is not long, so snow does not ball on it, as it does on some dogs and sheep, but simply falls off. Someone has calculated that reindeer have 2,000 hairs per square centimetre. I have to admit that I have never tried to verify this, but I do know that our reindeer never seem to be unduly bothered by the cold.

Each hair on a reindeer's body is hollow, affording maximum insulation, and the coat is very dry in texture, not oily. Expert swimmers, reindeer can be immersed in raging torrents during their summer migration yet shake themselves dry in seconds. Unlike other animals, reindeer's hair even extends under their feet (as a non-slip aid) and over their noses. It is their warm, dry, furry noses that make reindeer such a delight to feed by hand.

A furry nose is extremely important during the depths of winter. Pushing down through snow to find food would almost certainly result in frostbite if the skin was hairless, as in other animals. And, as we know ourselves, warm air exhaled from the lungs will condense and freeze on a cold, wet nose in sub-zero temperatures. Even in northern Siberia, where the temperature can plummet to a mind-numbing minus 60 °C, the reindeer's nose stays warm and dry and never freezes.

We once had a calf with quite the opposite problem: Flint was born a slate grey colour with a white flash on his forehead and white fur on his nose. Because white hair has less protective pigmentation underneath, poor Flint was terribly susceptible to sunburn, his nose appearing to receive the brunt of it. Come to think of it, perhaps he was just ambitious and thought a sunburnt nose was a good career move for an apprentice Christmas reindeer!

The hollow structure of reindeer hair makes it an incredibly effective insulator, rather like the hollow fill used in duvets. When reindeer lie down in the snow their body warmth cannot escape – if you examine the bed of snow where they have been lying, you will find that it is perfectly dry.

In addition, through the blood supply to the legs, there is a cunningly devised counter-current system, whereby blood vessels going to the extremities of the limbs run alongside blood vessels coming away. This results in warm blood being cooled on its way to the colder regions and cool blood being warmed before it reaches the main body mass: another great way of combating heat loss.

What reindeer eat has been a subject of research for many years and the introduction of reindeer to unusual places has led to some interesting results. For example, between 1911 and 1925 Norwegian whalers took a small number of reindeer to the island of South Georgia in Antarctica. Over the years the reindeer have increased; by 1972 the population had reached some 2,500 and today they continue to thrive, despite a lack of their traditional food, lichens. They cannot migrate, but graze throughout the year on the same food: tussock grass.

In Arctic regions, however, it is generally accepted that reindeer and lichens (also known as reindeer moss) go together like children and sweets. Reindeer simply love lichens. But what is the attraction? In the winter months in the far north, when thick snow covers their grazing, lichens are the only source of food that is still actually growing. This is because lichen is basically a fungus and fungi grow by absorbing nutrients from the ground and from atmospheric moisture, which means that, even in the absence of light, they still go on growing. However, within the body of the fungi are numerous single-celled green plants, or algae, that are able to photosynthesise when light is available. Each benefits the other and without each other they would not survive: a classic case of symbiosis.

Lichens do particularly well on thin, infertile soils, where normal green plants, with traditional root systems, are unable to grow due to lack of nutrients. In inhospitable Arctic regions, therefore, lichens predominate, which is of great benefit to the reindeer. High in carbohydrate and low in protein, they provide a perfect winter diet.

The carbohydrate provides the animals with instant energy during the long winter months. On the other hand, when protein is digested a toxic by-product, urea, is excreted via the urine, and the more an animal urinates, the more heat it loses. Thus, by feeding on a low-protein diet in the winter the reindeer excrete less urea and as a result cut down their heat loss to a minimum. Once the snow melts and the arctic summer hots up, lichens become less palatable. With no atmospheric moisture, they dry up and become hard and crisp to the touch and the reindeer then turn their attention to a much more varied and richer summer diet of birch, willow, grasses and sedges, rushes, mosses and mushrooms.

Lichens are slow growing so reindeer need to be kept in low densities on plenty of ground if the supply is not to be decimated – this is why our set-up in the Cairngorms is ideal. At our other base at Glenlivet, on the other hand, we have much less hill grazing, although the summer grazing is very good. There we have created two hill-grazing sites and we rotate the reindeer so that the lichens are not over-grazed.

When we have reindeer down at the house we usually pick some lichen to feed to them. During one very bad winter Wally, who was an orphan and was up on the hill with the herd, suddenly started to look poorly. Normally the cows do quite a lot of work for their calves in bad weather, digging for food for themselves and allowing the calf to feed from the same hole.

Without a mother to help him, Wally was unable to find food under the snow and became so weak that we decided to take him off the hill. The snow was so deep that *we* were not able to find any lichen, either. Lichen was clearly what he needed and we racked our brains as to what we could do. Then I remembered that in the exhibition room at Reindeer House there was a box of specimen lichens which Mr Utsi had picked some twenty years earlier. The marvellous thing about lichen is that you can re-hydrate it. So we simply wetted it with water and fed it to Wally. I am sure they were very special lichens, gathered for a good reason, but Wally was in great need and he was very much better for it.

Alan gives the reindeer far more supplementary feed than Mr Utsi used to, particularly in winter. Mr Utsi would probably not approve, but the reindeer do become much tamer when you feed them regularly and certainly grow much better antlers. And, of course, by feeding them you take a little of the pressure off the grazing.

The mix is much the same as that created by Mr Utsi, based on soaked sugar beet, maize and oats (Mr Utsi always used to carry Ryvita with him, too, when he was out on the hill – reindeer love Ryvita). Nowadays we use ready mixed feed called ewe-lamb mix but we still add wet sugar beet because reindeer can choke very quickly on dry feed.

Often when they reach us for their feed they have run quite a long way and are a bit puffed, so we never feed them as soon as they arrive. We count them, check them over and let them get their breath back, then put the feed on the ground. If we have visitors with us, we keep some back and everyone can hand-feed them. People love the sensation of feeding reindeer. With their wonderfully furry noses they tickle your hands and, since they do not have top front teeth, they cannot bite your fingers.

Food is certainly a great aid to herding reindeer, although their willingness to be herded does vary, depending on the time of year. On a cold, frosty day in mid-January, for instance, they can be called down off the hilltops from two miles away, hungry for the food they know you have for them. By contrast, during the height of summer, when natural food is plentiful, the air is heavy and they are being plagued by flies, they may take considerable persuasion to come.

One thing they are especially fond of is salt, and we always keep them supplied with salt licks. Their craving for salt seems to come from the fact that during the winter months they probably have a very low intake of minerals. Dr Lindgren told me that in Russia it was salt which attracted reindeer most, not supplementary feed. The tribes made their tents from salted skins and had to protect them from the reindeer, otherwise they would constantly lick them. It is interesting that in Scandinavia, where the reindeer migrate out to the coast in summer, they go down to the seashore and eat seaweed, so presumably they have quite a good natural intake of salt.

Provided they have the right food, then, reindeer can survive the worst winter climate in the world. When they do succumb to old age, it is usually because their teeth have worn down so much that they can no longer chew their food efficiently. Like other animals, reindeer grow a set of milk teeth which are then replaced by permanent adult teeth. There is a set of good molars at the back and, just like a sheep, at the front they have a hardened palate above and very small incisors at the bottom. This is why, provided you avoid sticking your finger in the back of their mouths (which is what Fiona did once when she was bottle-feeding a calf) they cannot bite you. Eventually, though, these teeth wear down and this is when, in the wild, old reindeer simply starve.

The average lifespan of a reindeer is about twelve or thirteen, perhaps a little less for a big bull. When a reindeer grows massive antlers, as bull reindeer tend to, there must be quite a redirection of calcium from the skeletal bone and presumably from the teeth, too, which probably makes the teeth wear down more quickly.

Culling is never easy, but we could never allow a reindeer to suffer a slow death through starvation. Once an old one starts to go downhill and stops putting on weight, we have to make a decision. Alan does it himself, using a humane killer. We would never allow our reindeer to be transported miles away to be killed in a slaughterhouse. When it is time, we bring the reindeer in question down off the hill on a halter and hand-feed it. It is all done very quietly and there is no stress to the animal. It is never easy taking the decision to put one down and I know that Alan really has to brace himself (though he would never admit it). But once it is over there is a huge sense of relief. You know that they have had a quick end, with no suffering, after a life spent in the habitat to which they are so perfectly adapted.

The extreme hardiness of reindeer is amply demonstrated by our herd during blizzard conditions on the Cairngorms. When the snow is drifting they never seek shelter in the lee of the hill, where they would ultimately be buried under snow. Instead they head out on to the exposed ridges where they can search more easily for food. Shelter from a storm is not a requirement, so while the

Reindeer calves are very precocious, on their feet (above) and following their mother immediately, an essential for survival in the wild. Below, they start showing signs of antler growth as early as three weeks.

Antlers are the fastest growing animal tissue. Above, Crackle in mid-June; his antlers have been coming since the beginning of March and are two-thirds grown; below, his full rack of antlers by the end of July.

Summer brings heat and flies, so best grazing (above) is in the early morning or late evening. By the time heather is in flower (below) the reindeer look at their very best, rolling in fat with long velvet antlers.

Mature bulls like Crackle (above left) are the first to strip their velvet. Above right, Pop is ready to take on all comers. Below, young bulls sparring, a game with serious undertones.

Halter-training for Christmas: above, did it really take three of us to catch Popeye for his first lesson? Right, he remains unconvinced. Reindeer hate to leave the herd. Below, a training walk down to Utsi's bridge. Popeye and Tundra followed Scapa like little steam trains.

When it comes to being fed on the hill, the reindeer love everybody.

The first to cast their antlers at the beginning of winter are the mature bulls like Gustav (above) who suddenly find themselves at the bottom of the pecking order. Below, reindeer will follow you right across the Cairngorms, as long as you're carrying a bag of food.

Above, Gustav, son of Troll, a real gentleman among reindeer and one of Alan's favourites. Below, alone with the herd. It is difficult to better these moments.

farmers are digging sheep out of snow drifts and throwing down extra silage for their cattle, we reindeer herders are warming our toes in front of the wood-burning stove.

When you next pass a field of cows, sheep or horses on a wet, windy day, note which way they are standing: it is most likely that they will have their backs to the wind. This of course blows their coats up and causes them to lose heat. Reindeer never do this. Watch reindeer in a blizzard and you will see that they face into the wind to keep the hairs lying flat and help trap more warm air through their coats.

Whenever we drive down the main A9 from Aviemore south through the Drumochter hills, with thick snow lying everywhere, we always see scores of red deer close to the road. In an effort to find shelter they end up in the glen, where the snow is deepest and finding food becomes even more difficult. I often muse that if it were reindeer occupying those hills, we should not see them because, with their much finer coats, they would never need to seek shelter.

I would love to see reindeer roaming throughout the Scottish Highlands but I know that it is unlikely ever to happen when there is already such a huge population of red deer and sheep. Yet reindeer are far better animals than sheep to have on the upland areas because they are much less destructive. I would also like to see the reintroduction of other mammals that once lived in the Highlands. The idea of reintroducing the wolf is tempting – though not for the reindeer – but I cannot see it happening. Throughout the world human beings are terrified of wolves. As soon as they come into contact with man they are persecuted and that is exactly what would happen in Scotland. On the other hand the lynx would be a smaller predator that could be acceptable. There would not be the same competition with man, because lynx generally prey on small mammals such as squirrels, weasels, mice and voles.

Although the Cairngorms provide perfect reindeer habitat, there will always be problems in herding reindeer on an area so much in demand for human recreation. The northern slopes, which is the area we lease for grazing, is intersected by Scotland's premier ski resort. The ski road winds its way up from the forest to a height of about 2,000 feet, where two car parks are to be found, capable of accommodating several thousand cars.

In the past we found that many of the inhabitants of coaches and cars were hell bent on enticing the reindeer closer with toast from breakfast, discarded sandwiches or half-eaten apples. This desire to feed animals indiscriminately is a selfish trait. The usual motive is to make the animal come closer, so that it can be touched or photographed. There is usually nothing altruistic in their actions.

One day, when Alan was coming down off the hill to one of the car parks, he found a small posse of reindeer hovering about a hundred yards above the road. Simultaneously, a woman in a car spotted them and screeched to a halt. Out jumped the occupants and the lady began rummaging in the boot of the car. Without revealing who he was, Alan stopped to pass the time of day. The lady told him that she had some cooked gammon to feed the reindeer. Alan gave her a quick run-down on the feeding habits of reindeer, suggesting that the gammon would be of more use to her than to them. One wonders what happened on the many other occasions, when no one was there to explain and save the reindeer from a totally unsuitable meal.

Two particular reindeer, Trix and Eros, were real ringleaders when it came to foraging at the car parks, encouraging other reindeer to follow them. They spent the majority of their time wandering from group to group, looking for food. Stories came back to us of Eros actually going into the ski lodge in pursuit of a meat pie. And one day a winter photograph of Trix, seen lying in a parking bay between two cars, appeared in the local newspaper accompanied by the the the caption: "This poor reindeer, driven by starvation, has overcome his fear of humans to look for food on the ski car park." In point of fact, Trix was merely ruminating in preparation for the next onslaught of exotic food on his stomach.

When Trix and Eros died, I am sorry to say that we almost flew the flag at Reindeer House. The current generation of reindeer have not learnt their reprehensible habits – long may it continue.

CHAPTER NINE

Reindeer, Take One

W hen I went to work as a reindeer volunteer the last thing I ever imagined I would be involved in was film making. But during our time at Reindeer House the herd have assisted, if only in a minor way, in a couple of notable productions. They have also been used in television programmes and a number of advertisements in which their performances surprised even us.

Santa Claus, The Movie was probably the closest we shall ever come to being personal advisers to Father Christmas himself. One autumn a representative from an American film company arrived for tea at Reindeer House to discuss with Dr Lindgren the possibility of hiring a number of reindeer. If he opened negotiations in the belief that large wads of money would do the trick he had certainly reckoned without Dr Lindgren. Apparently, she gave him a hard time. Unsuitably clad though he was, in smart pin-striped suit and highly polished shoes, the poor man was probably relieved to escape on to the open hillside with Alan to see the reindeer.

The film-makers were looking for two full teams of eight reindeer each, plus extras, and it soon became evident that we were were not going to be able to supply them with sufficient animals, which had to be roughly the same age and size. Eventually, they ended up going to Norwegian Lapland to find their stars. But before that happened Dr Lindgren negotiated with the company for Alan to go down to Pinewood Studios with two of our reindeer to assist in the making of models. The film people wanted to study them to see how they moved and how they fed and lay down to rest. This would then help them with the creation of life-size models which were to replace the real reindeer in all the close-up shots.

So, in February the following year Alan headed south in the company of Albert and Donner. Ever mindful of their welfare, Dr Lindgren insisted that he stayed with them for the entire time, while I remained at Reindeer House, doing my best to keep the herd under control and constantly digging cars out of snowdrifts. Receiving my first cheque from the film company with Santa Claus written on it cheered me up no end. I was so chuffed I photocopied it before paying it into the bank.

During the summer the Norwegian reindeer were brought in to do the actual filming and Alan and I went down to Pinewood to see how they were getting on. By the time we arrived they had been trained to harness and eight reindeer, harnessed up in four pairs one behind the other, was an amazing sight. To cap it all, every one of them had the most enormous antlers (they must have been stuffed with food to grow such spectacular ones). It was also a tremendous experience for us to go behind the scenes and see the working models based on Albert and Donner. Some were life-size, while others, for the flying sequences, were only toy-size. All of them were incredibly lifelike.

At the beginning of the film there is a scene with Father Christmas and Mrs Christmas returning home in the sleigh. They are caught in a terrible snow storm and the reindeer become too exhausted to pull the sleigh. They used models for that. When Dr Lindgren went to see the film she simply would not believe me when I told her they were models. She was totally taken in and truly believed that they had used real reindeer and made them collapse in the snow. She could not cope with that at all. Knowing how the film had really been made added greatly to our enjoyment of it. And at the end, when the credits came up, there was "The Reindeer Company, Aviemore", splashed across the cinema screen in great big letters. We felt very proud.

I have always felt rather sorry for the makers of the film because it was never quite the box-office success they expected. This was in no small part due to the fact that the media ran a story in which the film-makers were accused of slaughtering reindeer in order to make the models. In fact, it was truer to say that in buying animals from Norway, where thousands of reindeer are reared every year for meat, they had actually saved their lives. The skins which were used for the models came from reindeer that would have been killed anyway. Naturally, the whole experience made the producers very sensitive to adverse publicity and when the film was finished, because quarantine restrictions prevented the reindeer from returning to Norway and they could hardly shoot them all, they offered half of them to the Reindeer Company and the rest to the Norfolk Wildlife Park.

So we duly took delivery of ten *Santa Claus, The Movie* reindeer, who gloried in the names of Bronco Billy, Scruffy, Buddy, Jake, Sidney, Lawrence, Stubby, Gunner, Clement and Mouse. They were mature animals who had been born in the wild and, although they had been well cared for during their year in captivity it seemed that the sooner they could forget about life at Pinewood Studios the better. We kept them down at the house for a while, then integrated them into the herd on the hill. As they were all castrated males they were of no use to the herd as such, but it was good to see them returned to a natural life, and we did use one or two of them as Christmas reindeer, though they were never as tame and quiet as ours and were always on edge.

What did not occur to us at the time, having been surrounded by reindeer who had for several generations lived a settled life in the Cairngorms, was that come the autumn these Norwegian fellows would develop a strong urge to migrate, as they would in the wild. Various reports of stray reindeer filtered back to us. One ended up at Glenshee on the southern range of the Cairngorms. Sadly, he got no further and there was no opportunity to fetch him back because he was shot, apparently mistaken for a red deer.

Jake was another who headed south and west off the mountains, ending up in a field beside the River Spey. A phone call from someone living at Loch an Eilean alerted us to the fact that there was a reindeer on the move. We jumped into our little Renault van, together with a decoy in the form of Wally, and headed down to Rothiemurchus to look for him. We eventually found Jake, standing looking slightly bewildered in the middle of a field next to the river. Luckily, there were some empty steadings close by and after opening and closing a few gates we were ready to catch our stray. Wally was produced and Jake immediately ran across to greet his new-found friend. Alan then led Wally, with Jake tagging along behind, into the farmyard, while I scurried up to close the various gates. In these situations you only get one bite at the cherry so our adrenalin levels were well up. Fortunately, Operation Jake was successful first time and we were able to take him back to the herd.

Apart from providing us with some new reindeer, involvement with the film world had given Alan a whole new outlook on training and harnessing reindeer to pull sleighs. In the past he had always followed Mr Utsi's Sami methods, using a rope that passed between the animal's legs and was attached to the collar at one end and the sleigh at the other. The fact that a rope brushing against a reindeer's legs tends to make him jump around is of little consequence to someone travelling hundreds of miles over the tundra. A deviation of an odd mile or so is neither here nor there. But if you are in a crowded shopping-centre, the last thing you want is to have a reindeer hopping about all over the place.

So Alan studied and photographed the film reindeer harness, which had been specially designed by American animal-trainers, and adapted it for our use. In the studios the reindeer were harnessed in pairs. This has its advantages beause reindeer, being social animals, work better with a partner they can see. Use one on its own and he will invariably spend most of the time turning round to see where his friends have gone. This is why at our early Christmas events we always used to take an extra reindeer to walk beside the one pulling the sleigh.

However, the most important difference between Sami harness and the film-makers' harness was more fundamental than that. Alan had always used simple Lappish-style halters, which fastened round the back of the reindeer's neck, with a second strap round the base of the antlers and around the front of the forehead. The lead rope was then attached below the cheekbones. Because of the lack of a noseband, one had no control over the reindeer's noses, and so no way of preventing them throwing their heads about. Following the lead set by the film-makers, we replaced these halters with pony headcollars which are fitted with a noseband. Dr Lindgren was not impressed. She felt that the noseband was a retrograde step and an ugly addition to the reindeer's face. But, from a practical handling point of view, it was a great step forward.

Armed with Alan's new knowledge of harnessing techniques, I went to the saddler's in Inverness to buy some hessian girths, while he constructed the traces. We then practised harnessing up two Christmas reindeer side by side to the same sleigh – and what a difference it made. As a result we gained a lot of confidence in presenting reindeer and when the BBC got in touch during the winter of 1986 to say they were doing a serialisation of *The Lion, the Witch and the Wardrobe* from C. S. Lewis's *Chronicles of Narnia* we had no hesitation in agreeing to supply four reindeer harnessed to a sleigh.

The filming was done in the heart of the Glenmore Forest. The production team must have performed a very effective snow dance before their arrival, because during the three weeks of filming they had just what they wanted: deep snow covering the ground and hanging thick on the trees. It was a wonderful setting. In the book the White Witch's sleigh is pulled by two white reindeer, but pure white reindeer are rare and at the time we did not have any suitable ones, so white horses were used instead. However, our reindeer were perfect for the scene where Father Christmas arrives to say winter is over and Christmas is here. Our only worry was that filming was taking place quite late in the winter and many of our reindeer had already cast their antlers. Fortunately, we managed to get together a suitably antlered foursome, Keith, Albert, Norton and Jake.

The forest was alive with activity: everywhere there were cameramen, assistant cameramen, sound men, make-up people, not to mention a most impressive mobile canteen serving on-the-spot three-course meals for everyone. Four-wheel-drive vehicles were constantly going to and fro, when they were not getting stuck in the soft snow, that is. Human-sized beavers waddled around in impractical-looking costumes, make-up people fussed over Father Christmas's beard or the hang of the fur coats worn by the children. A distraught director seemed to have it in for poor old Father Christmas, who could not get his lines or the emphasis right. The reindeer were remarkably patient during take after take. Luckily, no one tried to re-arrange their appearance – I think they were too respectful of their antlers to get close enough.

At lunchtime everything came to a shuddering halt as the production team and actors leapt into the fleet of vehicles and were whizzed off to the canteen. We were left standing in the snow with four hungry reindeer. But we had not been forgotten. A quarter of an hour later a chap turned up with two trays of food: roast duck with all the trimmings. We had quite a feast. There was nothing for the reindeer though. Lichen must have been "off" that day. Luckily, we had brought some with us.

In between these two filming commitments, some of our reindeer were asked to appear in a different guise, one that was more in keeping with their natural behaviour – in theory at any rate. For the opening scene of *Spies Like Us* the producers wanted to film reindeer grazing peacefully in the Siberian forest. Suddenly there would be a tremendous noise and a nuclear warhead would be seen being towed through the forest by an enormous truck. The reindeer would be startled and run off. The edge of Glenmore Forest became Siberia and Alan constructed an enclosure so that when the reindeer "ran off" they ran somewhere they could be regrouped for subsequent shots, as necessary. The day was perfect, with a good covering of snow, and when Alan brought a group of reindeer down to the location they began to graze happily.

The only difficult part was actually getting them to look disturbed and to run. They are a pretty laid back bunch at the best of times and at first nothing Alan did, no amount of shouting and chasing, could take their minds off the serious business of eating. Then, suddenly inspired, he went off to the house. When he came back he was wearing Dr Lindgren's Manchurian wolf-skin coat (the pungent one she used to sleep in) and had his little terrier, Sky (Fly's successor), at his heels. Working on the principle that the two things which reindeer fear most are wolves and dogs, Alan and Sky hid in the trees and then, on the word "Action", leapt out at the reindeer. Dear old Keith, Albert, Donner and Jake and their friends looked suitably alarmed and the three-man camera crew went away happy. Could we have hoodwinked them a second time, I wonder, or had the reindeer rumbled Alan's disguise? Keith and Albert and co were not letting on but it was perhaps as well the shot was "in the can" first time.

On another occasion the BBC TV Natural History Unit from Bristol turned up to film reindeer foraging in the snow for a documentary, *The Living Isles*. To make sure the reindeer performed as required we buried small heaps of feed in the deep snow, knowing they would be unable to resist. They found and devoured the food in no time at all and were soon heads up looking for more. The film crew wanted another take, so second time round they concentrated on one particularly greedy reindeer, Oban. This time they decided to submerge the camera in the snow, bury the food close beside it and film Oban's foot at close quarters as he dug down through the snow to reach the food. As the cameraman put his eye to the viewfinder of his expensive piece of machinery, we released Oban.

Reindeer dig through snow very quickly, with a sharp, striking action, and you have to be fast to capture it on film. Oban reached his prize, scoffing it within seconds. Then, lifting his head, he suddenly noticed the intruder inches from his nose: in true reindeer style down came his front hoof, crack!, on top of the cameraman's head to move him on. We did not know whether to laugh or cry. It must have hurt a lot. Not surprisingly, he did not try that particular shot again.

The producer, wanting to make the most of the filming

opportunities that day, racked his brains for alternative ways of getting similar shots. Alan came up with a suggestion he had not been expecting. Buried in the deep freeze at Reindeer House are many strange objects. Normally, at the bottom, there is a collection of reindeer leg bones, complete with hooves and skin. We delved for a suitable specimen. Having observed reindeer feeding for many years, Alan had no difficulty in imitating their digging action. Hunting for food with the frozen foot in his hand, he completely stole the show. How we laughed when we saw the close-up on TV.

More recently we were asked if a natural history crew could film a reindeer calving. They were producing a film about migrating caribou in Alaska and since caribou are totally wild it was impossible to get close enough. One of our tame reindeer would be just the ticket – or so they thought. We arranged for them to arrive around May 12–13, at the height of the calving season.

On the first morning the crew were very keen, setting out at 3.30 a.m. just at first light. It was cold and snowy and there was a thick mist. One of the cows, Stream, had shown signs of being about to calve by breaking away from the herd the previous night, so we went looking for her. On the way we found Ferrari, who must have calved last thing the previous night. That was really too late for the crew and anyway the calf was a bit light in colour to pass as a wild caribou. So we continued our pursuit of Stream.

We found the entire herd, including Stream, on Silver Mount and the crew took some shots of them in the snow. Then, as we watched, Stream dutifully started to head off on her own. What luck. We began to follow her, little knowing what a merry dance she would lead us. Off she went through the deep, wet snow and the thick mist, lying down, getting up again, moving on and on until, at 9 a.m., we eventually lost her and came away, thoroughly despondent. To make up for their disappointment the crew filmed the herd again during the afternoon. Inevitably, while they were doing so Stream contrived to hide herself away and calve. As did Mantle. We began to think our reindeer were not so tame after all – at least not at calving time.

The following morning the crew were not quite so eager. They slept in, eventually meeting up with Alan on the hill. There they filmed Mantle's very small, tottery calf. But still they had no shots of an actual calving. Afterwards everyone went in search of Talisker, who had decided to detach herself from the herd. But again they were out of luck. She led them twice round Silver Mount before losing them completely and eventually heading back to the herd. After lunch they tried yet again, focusing this time on Walnut, who had also shown promise of calving. But again, nothing. Then the snow began to come down again in earnest and everyone beat a hasty retreat.

By the third morning a very weary television crew decided to stay put in their hotel, asking if I would ring them should anything happen. Typically, of course, everything did happen – all at once. We had kept back some cows we thought most likely to calve in a small fenced-off area. By the time I reached them Walnut had virtually calved and a number of others, having been held back overnight, were hankering to be let back out into the main enclosure. Compassion getting the better of me, I decided to let them out before heading down to ring the TV crew.

As I opened the gate and the reindeer began to filter out, I suddenly realised that Cherry was in the very process of calving: the calf's legs were already sticking out and it would all be over in no time at all, and here was I letting her out. The film crew had already made it quite clear that they did not relish another tramp round Silver Mount, so I tried to coax her back through the gate. But she was having none of it. Her mind was set on finding a nice dry spot in which to calve.

I scuttled down to Reindeer House, rang the crew and told them to come straight out and start filming. By the time they arrived Walnut had finished calving. With fingers crossed we headed out to look at Cherry. She was still with the herd but obviously in the throes of calving. She was lying slightly away from the grazing group, whose presence I think helped us to get in close. Cameras were set up and twenty minutes later it was all happening. The calf began to appear, hung for a moment, its hips apparently stuck, and then slipped out. Suddenly it was all over.

At last. The crew had everything they wanted. In fact they had more than they could have hoped for. Once Cherry had calved, they were able to get in really close and take some great shots of the calf staggering to its feet for the first time. The whole scene was shot in deep snow, with perfect light and a lovely, quiet female as the star of the show. Cherry's very first calving had been recorded for all time – and she had made the film crew's day.

Reindeer have also been hired to appear in commercials, a different experience again. An animal-trainer we know set up one for us with Italian TV. It was shot at Shepperton Studios and was for Nutella chocolate spread. They needed two reindeer to film three separate scenes. In the first the reindeer, harnessed to a beautiful sleigh, were required to deliver Santa to a snow-covered house and wait for him to alight, go down the chimney and deliver his presents, then come down off the roof again and jump back into the sleigh.

The producer wanted the reindeer to look up at Santa as he approached. Now getting reindeer to act was a completely new departure for us but we devised what we hoped would be a foolproof plan and hoped for the best. Alan was down on ground level, and I climbed up the "roof" – a very tall step ladder. On the word "Action!" I called to Gustav and Marble. In unison they swung their heads round to look at me. Then Alan called them and they swung their heads back to look at him. Then I called them and again they looked up at me. I am not sure who was more surprised, us or the producer. There was certainly a big smile on the face of our friend the animal-trainer who had recommended us. The reindeer had earned their bread in just two takes.

In the second scene Santa was throwing his sack of presents on to the sleigh and the reindeer were supposed to look back at him. The director suggested that Santa called them himself, but the reindeer simply ignored him. So we were again roped in to call them and again they performed perfectly.

The following day the idea was to film the reindeer flying. Well, that was asking too much, even of reindeer as talented as Marble and Gustav. In reality they had to run about thirty yards down a set, with blue sky behind, and the camera panning down so that it looked as if they were flying over the roofs of the houses. Our problem, as always, was that we never normally ask the reindeer to run ahead of us. We always lead them and so we become their link with the herd and they look to us for all their commands. The big question was, would they go anywhere without one of us to lead them?

We decided that Alan should go well ahead of them, out of shot, while I stayed at their heads and talked to them until the camera was ready for action. Fingers crossed, we got into position. And, miraculously, when I let them go and Alan started to run, off they went like the clappers. He really had to move to stay ahead of them.

Fortunately we had warned the crew to have a couple of men behind the sleigh just in case they set off in earnest. It took three stagehands hanging on to a steel cable attached to the sleigh to slow them down. In typical reindeer fashion, though, after a few takes they had it down to a fine art, setting off at a good lick when I let them go, and screeching to a halt at the far end at just the right moment. We had started the session not knowing quite whether Gustav and Marble were really up to this acting lark, but they had done us proud.

After that we were booked to do another commercial, this time for Citroën cars on French TV. They wanted four reindeer harnessed up to a sleigh standing on a thirty-foot turntable. The set was completely white and the reindeer had to stand surrounded by little elves with fake snow blowing at them while the turntable revolved. Gustav seemed to be the only one with any imagination. As soon as the turntable started to move, he was all for moving off too. Marble was keen on doing exactly what his old acting partner was doing, while Johan and Mackerel could not have cared less. It certainly was a weird feeling as the turntable moved round against the white background, but after we had rehearsed it a couple of times with us standing beside them they soon got used to it and when the cameras started rolling they were fine. The great thing always in these situations is to stay calm. Alan is so in tune with them, so placid, that the reindeer remain placid, too. In fact the only thing that ever bothers them in the studios is the heat. With all the lights it can become too much for them. Then we have to give them a break and take them outside for a rest and to cool off.

There is no doubt that the more we work with reindeer the more we realise what amenable and versatile creatures they are. There are still one or two things that they cannot do, however. One day we had a call from an ad. agency specialising in animals. The conversation went along the following lines.

"How much would it cost to bring a reindeer to London?"

"What for?"

"To do some still photography."

"We always take two."

"That's okay. I want the reindeer sitting down."

"Reindeer do not sit down."

"I've made other deer sit down for a photograph." The voice was vaguely familiar and I began to wonder if this was a wind-up.

"Not reindeer – they don't sit down."

"Okay, I'll have a dead one and stuff it in a sitting-down position."

"We don't have any dead reindeer."

"Well, I'll buy a live one and shoot it."

"We don't sell reindeer. Especially not to you."

"Well, what do you do with your surplus then?"

I felt like saying it was none of his business.

I was so bemused by the telephone conversation that as I headed off up the hill with the visitors I found myself visualising Gustav, dutifully sitting down on his haunches, looking across at me and wondering if he were doing the right thing...

We have heard no more from that gentleman.

CHAPTER TEN

The Smiths Go Joiking

Although our herd is of very modest proportions and our reindeer culture can be traced back for less than two decades, in September 1993 we were made to feel we really belonged, if only in a very small way, to the wider world of reindeer people.

Along with nomads from right across the northern hemisphere, we were invited to the First International Gathering of Reindeer People. Subsidised by the Norwegian Government and affiliated to the Fifth World Wilderness Congress, which took place simultaneously, the gathering met in the Arctic town of Tromsø and was attended by representatives of the majority of reindeer tribes.

By no stretch of the imagination could the Smiths of Reindeer House be described as a "reindeer tribe", but we do nevertheless live by our reindeer and we had no hesitation in accepting the invitation. Armed with cameras, warm clothes and our quota of duty-free alcohol (a friend having reminded us how expensive such a commodity is in Scandinavia), Alan, who had never been on a plane before, my father (a director of the Reindeer Company) and I took off from fog-bound Aberdeen to begin the trip of a lifetime.

The west coast of Norway looked truly spectacular as we flew north from Bergen to Tromsø over sea, fjords, mountains, glaciers and forests. Arriving at the airport, I diffidently asked a taxi driver for the Skipperhüset boarding house. Following my customary habit in such situations (in the ridiculous belief that foreigners will understand me better), I addressed him in broken English. He replied in fluent American.

Tromsø, we soon discovered, is very cosmopolitan and no wonder, for it is a most attractive place. It is situated on an island and surrounded by massive fjords, disappearing into mountains that rise above 6,000ft. They were still laden with the previous year's snow and looked magnificent. The air is crisp and clear, with a tremendous Arctic freshness. Being within the Arctic Circle, Tromsø enjoys constant daylight in the summer months. In the autumn, while we were there, the hours of light were very similar to Scotland. Of course the residents do have a price to pay for this wonderful environment: in mid-winter they have constant darkness for the best part of two months.

The venue for the opening ceremony of the Reindeer People's Gathering was the Fokus Cinema. Before the introductory speeches, representatives from all the reindeer breeding areas were lined up on stage for a photocall. I was the representative of the Scottish contingent.

Standing alongside all those people, dressed in their traditional costumes and with centuries of reindeer culture in their blood, I felt at first that I was intruding. Very much a product of the western world, looking well fed and at 5ft 6in noticeably taller than anybody else on stage, I could not help feeling out of place. Their knowledge came from a tradition that had been passed down through generations; mine had been learnt in a few brief years.

The colourful costumes of my companions looked wonderful. The Sami people's dress, different styles representing different districts, included heavily embroidered tunics and ornate head-dresses. These costumes appear to be worn only for Sunday best and have no practical function during the rest of the week. I believe, though, that they help the Sami people maintain their strong sense of tribal identity, both within their own culture and in the countries in which they live.

The reindeer people representing the Chukchi, Evenks, Nenets and Evens of northern Russia also wore traditional costumes. Some were predominantly of reindeer skins, incorporating the contrasting light and dark colour types. The borders of the coats were decorated with brightly coloured red and yellow felt. The women and children wore long coats, with reindeer skin boots, the men short tunics, skin trousers and ski boots. Other costumes looked somewhat less practical and, like the Sami outfits, are probably reserved for special occasions. However, all the styles reflected the inhospitable regions in which these people live. With their long coats, ski boots and brightly coloured head-dresses wrapped firmly round their faces, they looked ready to face even the longest winter of snow and sub-zero temperatures.

Many of the ethnic groups in Russia have all but lost their native language and all the reindeer people spoke Russian. Incredibly, though, this was the first time these people from northern Russia had all been together under one roof. The festival languages were Russian, English and Norwegian and representatives from each area went up on stage to give short presentations about their way of life.

The picture they conjured up was one of a vast expanse of mountains, tundra and taiga pastures, with a relatively small human population grazing huge numbers of reindeer. The land extends virtually unbroken from the west coast of Norway, above the Arctic Circle and halfway round the world to the Bering Strait. Over the entire area there are probably as many as two million semi-domesticated reindeer being herded and slaughtered for their meat, skins and antlers. A far cry from the Cairngorms.

We found, however, that the majority of these northern people no longer lead a traditional way of life: reindeer herding is becoming increasingly modernised. The Russians, in particular, bemoaned the fact that their children no longer herd reindeer, that traditional methods of milking and harnessing had all but been lost, that their cultural identity was under threat.

Some 60 per cent of the Russian land mass is occupied by people pursuing reindeer husbandry, yet current legislation does not even recognise it as a way of life. In fact, over the last hundred years the total number of domestic reindeer in Russia has declined by approximately one million, a reflection, perhaps, of the decline in the number of families actually continuing a life of reindeer herding. Perhaps, too, like our own agricultural industry, mechanisation and "progress" have led to fewer people being needed on the ground because they are simply not cost effective.

In contrast to Arctic Russia, the situation in North Scandinavia is quite different. In general there are too many domesticated reindeer being kept and this is leading to over-grazing and destruction of fragile habitats. The Sami no longer walk with their herds as they make their annual migrations. They now use helicopters, snow scooters and motorbikes. The reindeer no longer swim across fjords to their summer grazing on the coastal islands. They are loaded on to landing craft and ferried across.

Today's Sami seldom live in tents or keep a daily watch over their herds. Once the reindeer have reached their summer pastures, the men go back to their summer residence and do not see the reindeer again until early autumn, when they catch bulls for slaughter. It is not unknown for some herds to be moved between their summer and winter pastures by livestock transporters. The days of reindeer pulling sledges and being used as pack animals and for milking are all but over.

I doubt whether the Sami would wish to go back to the old nomadic lifestyle. Without doubt it was a very harsh existence and they can hardly be criticised for wanting the same home comforts enjoyed by other people in the western world. These one-time nomads are evolving ways to harvest their herds of reindeer without having to take the whole family along for the ride – and I suppose it is progress of a kind.

The results of research into reindeer and their grazing habits is increasingly being applied to their husbandry in an effort to prevent future misuse of the habitat. It will also provide the reindeer people with scientific evidence to support their way of life, which is more and more under threat from city-dwellers. Modern urban populations are totally divorced from the realities of everyday food production and of a culture that has evolved over thousands of years. Urban man is inclined to consider reindeer people primitive in their beliefs and ways of managing their herds. It is important for reindeer people to be able to demonstrate that reindeer herding is still a sustainable business in these Arctic regions, that over-grazing can be prevented by good land and herd management.

Having listened to a wealth of expert knowledge, I found it a hard act to follow when I was called up on stage to present the world of reindeer in Scotland. It had amused me, during the introductions, when the speaker described the present distribution of wild and domesticated reindeer: according to his world map, reindeer are distributed throughout Scotland. How could I make them comprehend that we made a living from just a hundred reindeer and that our herd did not migrate over thousands of miles of tundra or taiga but lived on a comparatively small part of a mountain range.

To get the message across, I likened our existence to that of a small nomadic family in Arctic Russia, who would keep a few reindeer and use them, not as a source of food, but as beasts of burden – as a means of moving the family from place to place while they are hunting and fishing. Extremely tame and well-handled, these reindeer would be extremely important to their way of life.

I explained that we know all of our reindeer individually, and see them daily; that many of them have been handled and halter-trained and about a quarter are trained to harness; that we have gained our knowledge from practical experience, supplementing it with any available literature and scientific papers that we could find. We live entirely by our reindeer, I told them. Without the herd our present lifestyle could not continue.

It was difficult, in just a few minutes, to get all the information across, to explain the history of the Cairngorm herd and our link with Scandinavia, to give a taste of our daily lives, the routine management of the herd and what we think the future might hold for us. But when I sat down I hoped that I had managed to put Scotland on the map in the eyes of the reindeer herding people of the world.

Before the festival, when the registration documents were being sent out, the children of reindeer herders were invited to submit drawings of reindeer herding to be judged by the festival participants in Tromsø. The drawings by children from the Russian contingent were particularly good and, on the whole, far superior to the rest. In many cases the children had not merely produced replicas of what they had seen but had used colour and shades to give an extraordinary impression of mood. Some incorporated a political message, too, questioning the future of their lifestyle in relation to other forms of exploitation in the areas where they lived. A good many of the drawings showed reindeer alongside helicopters and snow scooters.

There were quite a few children attending the festival and the following day's First World Championship Lassoing Competition began, appropriately, with classes for young people of various ages. I had wondered beforehand at the logistics of this contest. Would it be like *One Man and his Dog*? Would a group of reindeer be herded all day for the professional and amateur to attempt to lasso?

In the event it was nothing like that. No live reindeer came in contact with a lasso, in fact it made us wonder just how often these reindeer herders do actually use their lassos these days. The "reindeer" to be captured were mounted skulls, complete with antlers, lined up on a board alongside each other and about three feet apart. Contestants had to capture their quarry as many times as possible over a set time. Points were awarded for lassoing one antler, more points for both antlers, and minus points for two antlers from different "reindeer".

Some of the children, who were aged from about three to sixteen, obviously took it very seriously. Indeed among the Norwegian Sami, lasso-throwing is apparently a national sport. Deep concentration and determination gave victory to a teenage Sami girl.

Feeling that I had done my bit on the stage the day before, I chickened out from the women's section. Although one Norwegian Sami was very obviously out to win and had clearly put in plenty of practice, the majority of contestants were simply there to enjoy themselves. Two ladies from the Khanty-Mansi region of Russia, both very short and with weatherbeaten faces, were certainly game for a laugh – it must have been a long time since either of them had thrown a lasso.

Maria, the plumper of the two, was a renowned folk-singer in northern Russian circles. All of the singing, or joiking, we heard during the festival was unaccompanied.

Joiking stems from imitation of animal sounds and at first, at least to our untrained ears, sounded rather repetitive. There appear to be no actual words and it reminded us a little of yodelling. Sitting round a fire, doing household chores, joiking would probably help the hours to slip by pleasantly enough, but the two festival evenings devoted to a joiking concert seemed rather excessive. I still brought back a CD, though – for future reference.

It transpired that Maria's companion was a hunter. As a rule it is only the men of the tribe who hunt, but single women, who have no man to hunt for them, do join the hunting parties. Her achievements were considerable. The story was that she had killed sixteen bears in her life. Presumably being such a successful hunter gave her, as a single woman, tremendous status in her tribe.

When it came to the men's lassoing contest Alan bravely decided to enter. It was a well-subscribed competition and there were a variety of lassos in use. The traditional ones – which quite a few of the Russians used – are crafted from leather and antler but the modern versions are made of plastic-coated rope, with a plastic toggle. The modern version was on sale on the day of the competition and many entrants, including Alan, decided to purchase this latest development in lasso technology.

Once the men had shown their skill in lassoing the static reindeer, things really hotted up with the introduction of a moving target, the "reindeer" being fixed on to the ends of long rotating arms. The winners were announced during the evening at one of the many reindeer banquets which we attended. Each participant received a certificate proclaiming their name and the position in which they finished. Alan can now proudly add twelfth place in the first ever Lassoing Championship of the World to his other athletic feats.

The banquets were a carnivore's paradise, each

revolving around lumps of reindeer meat, and plenty of it: boiled ribs, steaks, tongues, marrow, dried strips, smoked blood pancakes and blood pudding. The accompaniment was without exception potatoes. As for the sweets which followed, they were out of this world, invariably involving cloudberries and cream. Cloudberries look like apricot-coloured raspberries. We find some growing in the mountainous region of Scotland but in northern Norway they grow in great abundance. They are delicious.

After spending three days in Tromsø and seeing only one reindeer we were keen to get into the field and find out what real reindeer country was like. Norway in autumn is truly spectacular, with the vast expanse of golden brown birch, extending from sea level to the mountain tops. We found that all the plant life we saw was familiar to us, the only real difference from Scotland being the comparative scarcity of the ling heather which gives the Scottish hills their distinctive purple sheen in August. It does grow in Norway, but not in such abundance.

A bus took us from Tromsø to Kautokeino in the heart of the reindeer's winter-grazing country. As we travelled further inland the terrain became flatter, with an abundance of birch trees and lichen. The reindeer were still out on their summer pastures, so unfortunately we did not see great herds on the move. However, there were small groups in the distance and we scored a point or two by being the first to spot them – no one else had brought binoculars or telescopes.

Communicating with the reindeer people from Russia became easier as time went on and we learnt to recognise the translators. Conversations via a translator were of necessity rather childlike but with perseverance we managed to convey what we hoped would be interesting information. Luckily, we had taken a lot of photographs with us, which instantly told a story and which we passed around while we were on the bus. With our mere one hundred reindeer we might have seemed something of a laughing stock when we arrived, but I think our companions were beginning to realise just how much contact we have with our herd and how well we are able to handle them.

Our bus journey ended at Kirkenes, on the Norwegian–Russian border, where we ate yet another reindeer meal provided by the local hotel. There was yet more pomp, ceremony and the making of presentations, although time was short that evening because most of the participants were setting off back into the Russian interior.

The spokesman for the Chukchi people from the Bering Strait stood up. He wanted to make one final presentation, "to the people with least culture but most commitment". And he asked one of us to step forward.

I felt incredibly honoured, and not a little emotional, as I walked up, watched by all those knowledgeable faces, and was given a beautiful ivory talisman made of walrus tusk. Vladimir said he hoped it would bring good luck and lasting prosperity to Scotland's only herd of reindeer. Informally, we were given other beautiful hand-crafted items and also bought various reindeer artefacts to remind us, along with our photos, of a tremendous experience.

On our return, with time to reflect, we could fully understand why Mr Utsi had decided to reintroduce reindeer into the Scottish Highlands, for the region is a miniature Arctic Norway. The only difference, as far as vegetation is concerned, is the lack, in Scotland, of naturally regenerative birch and pine woodland and high-altitude tree scrub. But then in north Norway the only major browsing animal is the reindeer, of which there are some quarter of a million, while the Highlands of Scotland support the same number of red deer, plus roe deer and sheep. And for every sheep there are seven rabbits. No wonder we have lost our tree layer.

CHAPTER ELEVEN

Napoleon and Friends

S ince buying the Reindeer Company in 1989 the biggest excitement in our lives has undoubtedly been the totally unexpected acquisition of thirty-eight new reindeer from France, which has provided an invaluable infusion of new blood into our herd.

In December 1994 we received a letter, quite out of the blue, from a man named Pierre Marc, owner of La Valleé de Renne in the Jura mountains. He told us that he was no longer able to keep his small herd of reindeer and would like to offer twenty-five of them to us as a gift. We had never heard of him, but he apparently knew of us through a friend who had once visited our herd.

Years back Pierre Marc had become enamoured of the Lappish way of life and in the early 'seventies had imported reindeer from Kautokeino in Norway and later from Finland to set up a herd at his home on the French–Swiss border. During the winter he took visitors to see the herd, part of the attraction being the provision of snow scooters to reach the reindeer enclosure up in the mountains. Now, however, the area had become a national nature reserve and snow scooters were banned. This had rather pulled the rug from under his feet: there was no longer an income to help support the reindeer and, with considerable regret, he had decided he must part with them.

I rang him to say we would be delighted to accept his offer, subject to importation requirements, and immediately got in touch with our local veterinary office.

The paperwork seemed relatively straightforward. The reindeer had already been tested for TB and there was apparently no problem with the rabies vaccinations which they had been given. So I wrote to Pierre Marc to tell him what would be required at his end. Then for several months we heard nothing.

We were just beginning to assume that it had all fallen through when, at the beginning of April 1995, we received a letter asking if we could take the reindeer by the end of the month. I went back to the veterinary office in Inverness and asked how quickly we could move, bearing in mind that calving time was fast approaching (we could not risk the cows calving en route) and the bulls would soon be growing their antlers. Inverness referred us to the Scottish Office in Edinburgh, but their premises were being refurbished and the senior veterinary officer was away on holiday.

Panicked because of the lack of time, I really rattled their cage, demanding a speedy answer. A week later they came back to us saying that it was nothing to do with them! As the reindeer would be landing in England it was an English problem and we should get in touch with the appropriate office in Tolworth, London. By now it was the second week in April and I was beginning to do my nut. Fortunately I found a very efficient contact in Tolworth, who got in touch with Inverness for details and quickly set about the preparation of the necessary documents. Pierre Marc was also incredibly helpful in getting health certificates sorted out at his end.

Things finally came to a head on Monday, April 24. The paperwork had been completed but now we were unable to arrange transport. Pierre had upped his original offer of twenty-five reindeer to thirty-eight, the entire herd, and they were going to need quite a lot of room, especially with the cows being in calf. I contacted someone who specialises in importing deer but he could not do anything before May 4, which would be too late. He explained that because of the protests against live animal exports from British ports, quite a few firms had pulled out of the international transportation business and those which remained were chock-a-block with work.

In desperation I rang Pierre Marc to ask if there was anything he could do at his end. Luckily, he managed to find a French haulier with two articulated lorries, one forty-eight-foot long and one forty-foot. Perfect. Alan and I, together with our assistant Janet and a friend, jumped into the car on the Thursday night, drove all night to London, picked up the import licence in Tolworth, and continued on down to Portsmouth to catch the ferry to Le Havre. We reached Le Havre at 9 p.m. and again drove all night, arriving in the Jura mountains at six o'clock the next morning. Exhausted, we fell into bed, only to wake an hour later, too excited to sleep.

The hauliers were due at ten, so we met up with Pierre Marc beforehand and went to look at the herd. It was an extraordinary sensation to look at those reindeer and realise they were about to become ours. Pierre explained his management system and showed us the herd's summer grazing. Because they lived in a relatively confined, fenced-off area, they had always received far more supplementary feed than our reindeer and we would have to introduce them gradually to our grazing and feeding system so as to avoid upsetting their digestive systems. Accordingly, we acquired a ton of the pellets that they had been receiving to carry them through the transition period.

Pierre clearly cared a great deal for his reindeer. He took us to see the barn to which they had access. Although the climate is similar to ours it does get hotter there at the height of summer and the herd needed more shelter from the sun. The barn had been fitted with three enormous fans and Pierre told us that on hot days the cleverest reindeer would lie down right in front of them.

Loading the reindeer into the lorries proved no problem at all as they were accustomed to being transported by road between their summer and winter grazing. We herded them into corrals and then down a little fenced corridor and in they went, the cows and calves in one lorry, the bulls and oxen in the other. The lorries had an ample supply of sawdust and deep straw beds so that the reindeer could lie down in comfort. There was loads of space for them all and room for us to water and feed them during the journey without having to take them out. The lorries also had extremely good ventilation.

It must have been a sad moment for Pierre Marc and his family as the little convoy set off that afternoon but he was remarkably philosophical. Getting the reindeer from Lapland had been a dream for him, he said, and now there was a happy ending to the dream. He knew that his reindeer were going to a good, caring home, and he promised to pay us all a visit later in the year.

The one problem which we had been warned might arise did not, in fact, materialise. Back in the December, when Pierre had originally made his offer of twenty-five reindeer, he had intended to sell the remainder to a reserve elsewhere in France. But when the buyer came to pick them up the villagers erected barricades and would not let the reindeer through. At the back of our minds was the nagging doubt that, having successfully arranged paperwork and transportation in record time, we would be stopped from leaving by a local protest. But the villagers must have resigned themselves to the loss of "their" reindeer. On the day only two young girls turned out. With tears in their eyes, they stood holding little banners saying "Please leave the reindeer". They made me feel like the big, bad wolf.

The journey went remarkably smoothly, back across to Le Havre and on to the eight o'clock ferry on the Sunday morning. The only nerve-racking part was approaching customs. Were our papers in order? Would we be stopped? Would there be a hold up? Over and over again I checked the documents and rehearsed what I would say if there were any problems. I need not have worried. The lorries were waved through. Nobody wanted to look inside them. And nobody asked to see my import licence. As I waved it somewhat frantically under official-looking noses, the rest of our little party told me to shut up and not complicate matters. So that was that. We carried blithely on our way.

Hoping that the French drivers would do the journey in one hop, we led them north through England, stopping a couple of times to check on the reindeer and grab a bite to eat ourselves. When we reached Hamilton we stopped again – we thought for another brief rest. But it turned out that the lorry drivers thought otherwise. They were going to bed down in their cabs for five hours. We had no option but to spend yet another night in the car.

Eventually we bowled into our farm at Glenlivet at mid-morning on the following day. Alan had prepared a pen for the reindeer. They came out of the lorries, looked around them, took a deep breath of Scottish air – and have never looked back. There had been no casualties and no cows had calved. Next day the divisional veterinary officer turned up to carry out a post-import inspection, and he pronounced the newcomers fit and well.

They settled in remarkably quickly and have taken the change of diet in their stride. A gradual switch from their customary concentrated feed to ours caused no problems and grazing them on heather moorland meant that not a lot could go wrong there; anyway, having been kept on Alpine pasture they are, I suspect, better adapted to grassland than our reindeer.

We immediately began encouraging them to come up to us and feed from our hands. They were already very used to people but Pierre Marc had handled them more in the traditional Lappish way. He would throw a rope round them, put on the harness and just go. We needed to get them used to our method of putting an arm round their necks and slipping a halter on. Whereas he wanted them to run, we want them to stand patiently.

Although Pierre had given one or two of the reindeer names there had not been time for us to learn them or study their characteristics. So we started again from scratch, choosing French names for each of them, beginning with the number one bull whom we christened Napoleon.

The males of the herd are a wee bit bigger than our reindeer. Pierre said a Lappish family whom he had got to know very well told him they thought his calves were a little bigger than theirs and thought it was probably because of the pellets on which he fed them ad lib. Unfortunately, I did not have time to see any of his antlers – they are always a good indication.

After calving we started splitting off some of the young French reindeer and integrating them with ours, both at Glenlivet and at Cairngorm. We shall cross our bulls with the French cows and the French bulls with our cows. I had always hoped one day to be able to bring more reindeer into this country. But the quarantine, which was only a few weeks in Mr Utsi's time, is now six months and it would have been an expensive undertaking. Apart from anything else, we would have wanted to see the reindeer first to make sure of what we were getting.

Fortunately, Mr Utsi's original herd came from tremendously diverse backgrounds – north Sweden, Norway and Russia – so we were not having to eke out poor bloodlines and there was certainly never any sign of the classic results of inbreeding: very low fertility rate and very small calves. But this new blood from the French herd is more than welcome. It will set the herd up for many, many years to come. What is more, the arrival of the French reindeer took our total number of reindeer to 144 and that was before the 1995 calving season had even got underway. It is a dream come true for us, too. How Mr Utsi would have loved to see it.

CHAPTER TWELVE

Great Ambassadors

Reading back through the records at Reindeer House I came across a marvellously succinct remark of Mr Utsi's about one of the bull reindeer imported in the early days. It said simply: "Jacob – very friendly bull. He'll kill you in the rut."

When you live in close proximity to reindeer you find, as with any other animal, that their personalities vary just as much as humans'. Some are timid, some are inquisitive, some are bold, some are aggressive, some are downright greedy, some are incredibly tame. Often, as in the case of Jacob, it is the tamest who are the most aggressive, simply because they have no fear of you. No reindeer is more friendly than the orphaned calf, for whom, of course, you become a surrogate mother. And as Mr Utsi discovered back in the early 1960s, no reindeer becomes more of a handful than a grown-up, friendly, hand-reared bull.

One such character was Boko, reared by Mr Utsi from a few days old. Boko became a delight. Like a faithful dog, he followed Mr Utsi everywhere. On shopping expeditions to Inverness the pair were inseparable. On one memorable occasion, when Mr Utsi was travelling south to Cambridge with Boko, he booked himself into a hotel for the night. As he crossed the reception area, with Boko as usual in hot pursuit, the manager accosted Mr Utsi, saying that he could not take a "goat" up to his bedroom. Affronted more by the fact that the manager had mistaken his beloved reindeer for a goat than by anything else, Mr Utsi promptly left. I doubt whether he patronised that particular hotel again.

Unfortunately, as Boko matured into a young bull he became more of handful. His desire to investigate the insides of rucksacks, not to mention cars, meant that he made frequent sorties to the ski car parks. When out on the hill he would boldly approach unsuspecting walkers to find out what they had to offer by way of food. His total lack of fear and insatiable desire for tit-bits, combined with the fact that he had matured into a full-size bull, ensured that in time his reputation went ahead of him.

Ove was another lovable, very friendly reindeer. A beautiful big, black bull, he had one undesirable habit. Most visitors to the herd arrive wearing trousers. But just occasionally someone does turn up in a skirt – an elderly lady, for instance, might come on to the hill in a smart tweed suit. And that was what Ove would be waiting for.

Off you would go, up the hill. The reindeer would come and people would be feeding and photographing them and then, all at once, there would be a shriek from the back of the group and you would know that it had happened again: Ove had lowered his antlers and whipped up the lady's skirt. He was not being aggressive, he was just being naughty. And I am absolutely certain that he did it on purpose because he clearly enjoyed the reaction it produced.

When the day arrived that the Highland Wildlife Park down the road needed a new bull, we decided that it had to be Ove: his embarrassing behaviour finally cost him his freedom.

Reindeer are naughty for different reasons. Some are simply cussed, others begin life quite nervous and shy and their only defence is to stand their ground and challenge rather than run away. Some, for example, develop an aversion to small children. As soon as they come within range, they smack them on top of the head with their feet. This can be slightly embarrassing when it is visitors' children on the receiving end.

Albert was a classic example. He was a big, tame Christmas reindeer with a big career drawback – a severe loathing for small children. He could pick them out a mile off. If Fiona and Alex ever wandered far from my side on the hill, he would be straight after them, chasing them. Because reindeer are not big animals themselves, he would never have seriously harmed them, but he could have biffed them over because they were so little. He was a nuisance with small children generally. You find it with other animals, too. I think it is because the animals are not quite sure what it is scuttling around at ground level. Perhaps a small child reminds them of a fox or other predator, so they decide to whack it down in case it gets them first. I tell visitors with small children always to keep hold of their hands, so that it is obvious to the reindeer that they are connected to something larger.

Cinnamon is a funny-looking reindeer with eyes that seem to pop out of her head. Her problem as far as visitors are concerned is that she is terribly protective towards her calves. If anyone comes up to her, or to her calf if they are separated, she will give them a jolly good hiding with her antlers. Her first calf was a dear little thing called Ruby who, sadly, did not survive. The visitors had fed the reindeer and we were all standing around chatting. One of the group spotted Cinnamon with Ruby, beautifully posed, and thought what a lovely picture they would make. So, in all innocence, she walked forward from the group, took her picture, turned round and strolled back. Three seconds later Cinnamon came burning up behind her, went bat-bat-bat-bat in her back with her antlers and then ran off again. It was as if she were saying "How *dare* you take a photograph of me with my calf!" The poor woman did not know what had hit her, though fortunately no great harm was done.

Other reindeer are just the opposite. They are so friendly that they are all over you. The number of times people have seen their cameras being transported away, dangling around a reindeer's antlers! Reindeer are good at knocking people's glasses off, too. Food is always a temptation for them to come too close, as Alex found out to his cost when he was tiny. We had just fed the reindeer and put the feed sacks down on the ground. Alex, in the typical investigative mood of a two-and-a-half-year-old, decided to crawl into a sack. One of the reindeer, Johan, could scarcely believe his luck when he caught sight of this unexpected bonus: a moving bag of feed. Reindeer are incredibly adept at opening feed bags with their feet and Johan set to work with great gusto. To my relief, Alex emerged unharmed. As far as I know, he never crawled into a feed bag again.

But when it came to love of food, there was no reindeer to excel Hannah. Always friendly and easy to catch, she was a delightful character. She had the face almost of a Jersey cow, with light colouring around her eyes, a dished (slightly concave) profile and a gentle look about her. With her well-shaped antlers, she always managed to look elegant. She lived to the grand old age of sixteen (over ninety in human terms) and remained youthful-looking until her very last year.

One morning she was happily laid up at the far end of the enclosure, apparently in the last stages of calving. Through the telescope we could see the calf's feet sticking out. Now this happened to coincide with feed time and we had come on to the hill with a small party of visitors. Calf or no calf, Hannah was not going to miss out on a meal. Hearing Alan call, "Lo-lo, come on now," and seeing the rest of the herd galloping over, Hannah instantly forgot about impending motherhood. Back in went the calf's feet and up she came with the rest. She proceeded to tuck into the food as if nothing was happening. Then, once she was satisfied that there was no more, she ambled some twenty yards away and calved in full view of the visitors.

There was only a single family on the hill that day. The mother and her two young children stood fascinated by the spectacle. The father, though, was not too sure. He started looking at his watch and muttering that it was getting late and "shouldn't we be getting back". Midwifery was definitely not his scene.

Females will breed literally until they drop dead. Natasha was a case in point. Normally reindeer start calving when they are three, but Natasha started as a two-year-old, which is about as good a record as you can get. She had her twelfth and last calf when she was thirteen. As usual she calved in the enclosure before going out on to the Cairngorms for the summer. As the months went by Alan noted that Natasha and her calf were missing. Then one day when he returned from the hill to his van he found a note on the windscreen saying that there was a baby reindeer wandering about in the ski car park. Sure enough, standing in the middle of the car park was a calf, about three and a half months old, all on its own and looking very lost. There were no other reindeer in sight.

Commandeering the assistance of a couple of walkers who happened to be coming down off the hill, Alan managed to catch the calf, put him in the van and drive him down to Reindeer House. At three and a half months a reindeer calf no longer needs to be bottle fed, so Alan shut him in the garden. But as soon as he went into the house the calf began to jump up at the window, desperately trying to get in. In the end Alan relented and the wee chap at once became calm and lay down. All that night, and for a few afterwards, he slept beside our bed – until, reindeer being impossible to house train, I put my foot down and Alan put him outside again.

A reindeer called Tiree had come down off the hill without a calf so the following morning we took the calf and stood it in front of her, thinking it might be hers. But she gave us a haughty look that clearly said, "That's nothing to do with me!" So we named him Mystery. And eventually, by a process of elimination, we worked out that he was Natasha's last calf and that she must have died on the hill during the summer. Goodness knows how Mystery had managed to reach the car park on his own – unless he had followed someone. If he had, and he had seen them get into their car and drive away, that would explain why he would not leave the car park. When Alan appeared he looked upon him as his saviour. He is still very attached to Alan.

Alan's all-time favourite, however, will always be a reindeer called Troll, who was born in 1978 (I suspect that Mr Utsi must have had quite a sense of humour: he named three of the bulls Trip, Trap – and Troll). Troll was a very proud reindeer, who enjoyed being dominant. When I first came to Reindeer House I quickly learned that one did not mess with him. In the rutting season he was a nasty piece of work, really ferocious. None of the other bulls matched up to him.

Troll was a big, heavy individual with a huge face and a big bulbous nose. He was very tame and very clever. When Alan first became herdsman it was the practice after the calving season to put the cows and calves out on to the Cairngorms to enjoy themselves and to put in their place in the enclosure a group of bulls – Christmas reindeer, young bulls, perhaps some cows that did not have calves. These were the reindeer that the visitors were shown during the summer.

Troll, however, was one bull who never came into the enclosure for the simple reason that he was never to be seen. Alan regularly scoured the Cairngorms but never found him. However, around the middle of August or beginning of September, when the rutting season was about to start, suddenly he would turn up, fat as butter. He would eye you and seem to say, "Ah, you don't know where I've been, but I've been having a good time." He would be looking very impressive, all set to beat the pants off any other bull.

In the past when we had a lot of bulls in the herd there was a tremendous problem with them getting caught up by the antlers on wire fences, so we used to saw their antlers off – a painless process once they have passed the velvet stage. If you cut one bull's antlers off, then of course you have to cut them all off, otherwise it leaves some bulls with an unfair advantage. The first year I was involved in this we made a big mistake: we cut Troll's antlers off before anybody else's. That meant that from being number one he promptly went to the bottom of the peck order. It took only a few seconds for Alan to realise how foolish we had been. Another bull, Gold, instantly summed up the situation and got ready to challenge Troll.

Alan quickly opened the nearby gate and let Troll through, slamming it behind him so that Troll was separated from the other bulls by the fence. But Troll was not having any of that. Having your antlers sawn off must be rather like taking off a pair of heavy boots – for a while you think you are still wearing them. Troll turned on a sixpence and hurtled smack into Alan and the gate. It was the only time that I have ever seen Alan caught off his guard.

In the winter Troll, like the other bulls, spent most of his time on Bynack More. If you wanted to move them elsewhere a call would bring them to you and you could slip a halter on one and lead the lot, an assistant chivvying them along from behind. In the spring of 1990 we had gone up to Bynack and found eight or nine males. But there was no sign of Troll, who by now was a very old reindeer. Alan scoured around for some time before he eventually found him. He looked dreadful: a walking skeleton, a complete bag of bones. He had evidently just managed to cling on over the winter, eking out a meagre living. We managed to join him up with the rest of the group and then attempted to herd them all together. But old Troll simply would not come. Under normal circumstances a reindeer who does not want to be herded in a particular direction will run off, breaking away from the main group. But Troll did not have the energy. Instead, every time Alan tried to round him up he turned and faced us. Every time we attempted to herd him towards the rest and down off Bynack More he put his head down and charged at us. He made it quite plain that he had no intention of moving.

With a lump in our throats we realised that we would just have to abandon him. If we had managed to take him home, we would have shot him to put him out of his misery. As it was, we had to leave him to face a slow lingering death. For a reindeer the ultimate fate, in the absence of a large predator such as a wolf, is to starve to death. With heavy hearts we headed off, thinking it would be the last time we would ever see him.

The summer progressed. Then one day a shepherd, Donny Smith of Nethy Bridge, rang to say he had spotted a single reindeer grazing on his hill. Alan thought it strange, as he believed they were all accounted for. He headed off to Donny Smith's, taking Gustav with him as decoy. Together Alan and Donny set off to where the stray reindeer had last been seen. And, when Alan called, who should coming running down but Troll. After we had left him for dead he must have returned to his customary secret grazing, for he was fatter than when we had seen him last and was growing his new velvet antlers. Together with

Gustav, who was probably his son (they look very alike), he jumped obediently into the van. I could scarcely believe my eyes when he jumped out at the Reindeer Centre.

After such a wonderful life as top reindeer, he eventually came to a sad end. A passer-by threw some dog biscuits over the fence and Troll picked them up. Oddly shaped, they stuck in his throat and he was unable to eat. So we had to put him down after all. It left us feeling that, in the end, we had not done him justice.

If I had to choose a favourite reindeer, it would be Beauty, aptly named by Fiona. In fact, she is the first favourite I have ever had. I always try to keep things in perspective, remember that they are all reindeer, but I must admit that Beauty is special.

I do not like bringing reindeer into the house too much. For one thing they tend to find life indoors too hot and in order to lose heat they urinate; for another, you have to go round picking up the droppings, though luckily reindeer droppings are rather like rabbits' pellets and are easily swept up. Beauty, however, was an exception. She used to come in a lot. She would even climb up on to the sofa and lie on my lap. It all began because she was orphaned when she was very small.

Her mother was Sorrel, a lovely reindeer who grew heart-shaped antlers and was very quiet and friendly. She calved for the first time on May 1, 1993 – the first cow to calve that year. The cows calve somewhere out in the 1,000-acre enclosure, but once the calves are born we like to bring them into a smaller, penned area, that we call a corridor, where we can keep a bit more of an eye on them. Foxes can be a problem when the calves are small, but you can combat it by bringing all the cows together, because a fox will not challenge a group of reindeer.

Normally, when a cow calves she is a bit edgy and will not let you touch her calf. Some do not mind but usually it is a question of herding them down to the corridor, just chivvying them along. Sorrel was an exception. She was so friendly that we simply put her on a halter and led her, with the calf trotting along beside her. She did not even mind when we picked up her little offspring. We took them down to the corridor and waited for the others to calve. Every day I would go and give her a feed and all was fine. Then, one day, Colin, one of our volunteers came down off the hill and said that Sorrel was really ill – on her last legs.

When I reached her she was unconscious on the ground, her little calf lying beside her looking at her pathetically. I called Andrew Rafferty, our vet, but there was nothing he could do. She never got up again and was dead in twenty-four hours. When we realised that there was no hope for Sorrel, I took her little calf down to the house. I had no trouble in feeding her. I had done of a lot of bottle-rearing of muntjac, and reindeer are very quick to get on to the bottle. The most important thing to remember is not to give them too much. This is why it is essential for bottle-feeding to be done by the same person, so that there is no question of the calf being fed twice. We use a dilution of Carnation milk, something which Mr Utsi had devised, and then, as they become older, they go on to a ewe-lamb reconstituted powder.

I quickly became hooked on Beauty. She became hooked on me in return, though I did try not to imprint her too much, putting her out into the paddock beside the house as soon as I could. Reindeer soon start eating solid food – they eat lichen when they are only a few days old – and she seemed to be doing fine. Every day I took her out to the heathery bank behind Reindeer House to give her the chance to browse on blaeberry leaves, heather shoots and grasses. She was given wet lichens and small handfuls of the same coarse mix that we give to the herd and we cut birch for her, since reindeer find the young leaves palatable. Then, all at once, when she was six weeks old she fell dreadfully ill. She became listless, ran a roaring temperature and became very weak. I summoned the vet, who injected her with antibiotics.

Mr Rafferty, sensing how upset I felt, was kindness itself and insisted on returning the next day to monitor her progress. At first she failed to respond to the antibiotics and it was three days before he found a successful treatment. By this time she was so weak that she could not stand up. But I did not give up hope, because although she could not lift her head off the ground she did, after some encouragement, take the bottle of milk. Fortunately, she seemed totally unstressed at being on her own, without the company of other reindeer. Eventually the antibiotics brought her temperature down. But when she began to get up again she was unable to walk in a straight line. Her head hung low and there was an ominous flickering of her eyelids. Mr Rafferty watched her and then told me he was afraid she had had some sort of meningitis and had suffered brain damage. I thought how unfair it was. I was so fond of her and now I had visions of having a "vegetable" reindeer around the place.

I was up at all hours of the night giving her the bottle and making sure that she never fell on to her side (it is very important that reindeer are not allowed to do this: they should never slump but should lie with their feet tucked under them). Beauty kept on taking the bottle and slowly, very slowly, showed signs of recovering – though for a long time she held her head to one side and staggered as she walked. Gradually, though, she became stronger and stronger, until eventually I realised to my joy that she did not have brain damage after all. She made a total recovery.

The only problem was that in doing so she ended up

dotty about me. Female reindeer have a tremendous bond with their mothers and she obviously thought of me as her mother. When I first introduced her back into the herd I felt awful – and visitors must have thought me a swine. When I went up the hill she would follow me everywhere. Then, when the time came to go, I would shut the gate and walk away and she would run up and down trying to follow. People would say, "How can you leave her like that?" I could only explain that it was best for her in the long run that she returned to the herd and lived the life of a reindeer, not of a pet. And she did learn to stay with the herd, at least in the summer when she was in the fenced enclosure. In winter, however, when the herd is on the hill she will not stay with the others but follows us down.

I used to try to escape by jumping in the car and driving off. But then I would steal back up to check on her and there she would be, directing traffic on the road, waiting for me. In the end I decided the best thing was for her to go over to Glenlivet, where she cannot follow people away. Also, I am not there every day to remind her who I am. So she will spend the winters there and come back to the Cairngorms in the summer.

When I go to the house at Glenlivet I only have to call her and she comes belting down to me. She lets me catch hold of her head and hold her – she is the only reindeer who will let me do that. Visitors love her and are always wanting to take photographs of her. The only trouble is that they always end up with my trunk-like legs in the picture, too, because Beauty insists on standing so close to me.

Wally was another orphaned calf, and the first that Alan hand-reared. He was the perfect Christmas reindeer, an ideal candidate for playgroups and children's nurseries at Christmas time when the excitement level is running high. He positively enjoyed human company and would seek it out in preference to that of other reindeer. Like Beauty, as a calf he was often in the house and as he got older we would always make sure that he came inside once in a while. Whenever he was invited in it was just like old times. He would carefully negotiate his antlers through the doorways and down the corridor and then settle himelf down on the sitting-room carpet.

Wally's mother, Princess, dropped dead when he was four days old. Alan took him to the house straight away and Wally very quickly became imprinted on his new parent. For the first few nights Wally slept beside the bed. Then he went outside. But if Alan failed to wake at the due time for his four-hourly feed, Wally's incessant grunting at the window eventually brought him out of the deepest slumber. Not surprisingly, Wally became very attached to Alan, almost to the point of jealousy if he thought other reindeer were attracting his attention. He was even jealous of me and would put himself between me and Alan when we were walking on the hill, threatening me with his antlers to keep me at bay. If anybody else got between him and Alan, he would jab them up the bum and move them on. He wanted to go everywhere Alan went and, like Beauty, did not like staying on the hill.

But when it came to getting off the hill he was much more ambitious than Beauty. One night he turned up in the feed shed at Reindeer House. I thought at first that Alan had brought him down. But no, Wally had done his own navigating. He knew exactly where he was going and after that he turned up uninvited quite a few times. In fact, he became quite a liability because he was always at the car park looking for Alan. One cold winter's day when we were preparing for Christmas we had caught Keith, one of our Christmas reindeer, ready for an event. Alan was leading the rest of the herd away on to the hill to feed them and was going to come back and put Keith in the van and drive down to the house. I was left on the ski car park holding Keith on a rope.

Wally was notoriously jealous of other reindeer being led on a halter, so he decided to forgo the attractions of food in order to sort out Keith in the car park. Normally I would have quite ably fended off a young bull but on this occasion there was sheet ice everywhere and I had Alex in a papoose on my back. Not wanting to fall backwards on top of Alex, I turned my back on Wally and hoped for the best. One of the golden rules when handling reindeer is "never let your reindeer go". If you do, they invariably head off in the opposite direction, never to be seen again. Keith, in his bid to escape Wally's hooves that by now were raining down on him, tried to pull away and managed to drag Alex and me to the ground. This of course gave Wally every opportunity to clobber us with his feet as well. Eventually I had to let Keith go and the two of them ran off to join the herd. Alan had one or two terse words with Wally, including the threat to geld him the following summer – which he duly did.

Wally became a bit of a ringleader, encouraging other reindeer to hang about the ski car parks. So, since we could not chase him off, in the end we sent him to stay with a very good friend of ours – though we still used him at Christmas time. Christmas without Wally would not have been the same somehow.

Our lives are inextricably entwined with the lives of our reindeer. The unstoppable process of calving, growing new antlers, surviving the winter continues regardless, and we worry for their welfare as if they were our own children. Dr Lindgren once said to me, "Mr Utsi lived for his reindeer by day and dreamt about them at night." Now I can well understand that. Visitors to the herd often look surprised when we explain we live by reindeer alone. If only they knew what went on for the other twenty-three hours a day!

Our herd are healthy and happy and the majority of them spend most of the year out on the hill where nature intended them to be. Only the Christmas reindeer are required to do "unnatural" things like visiting shopping-centres. But this is only for a few weeks of the year and their participation in the Christmas festivities does have a positive side. For they bring an awareness, however fleeting, of what reindeer are really like to people who will never have the chance to set eyes on one in the wild, even though they may claim to have seen one (usually a deer) in their garden. So they are helping to keep alive the ancient traditions of reindeer culture.

As for ourselves, at whatever time of the year we are always looking ahead, there is never time to dwell in the past as we count the cows that should be in calf, muse over antler growth and the size they will be by the end of the summer and organise events for the Christmas tour.

A lady from Dorset phoned recently. She had seen our reindeer at Ringwood last Christmas, she explained, and wondered what would be involved in hiring them for a Sunday in December. I explained what we provided, mentioned the cost and assured her there would be some available when she wanted, but urged her to confirm her booking soon as, even though it was only the end of May, the Christmas engagements were already coming in.

"Oh no, my dear," she explained. "I'm not thinking of *this* year. I want the reindeer for the millennium."

ADOPT A REINDEER
THE CAIRNGORM REINDEER SUPPORT SCHEME

Under the Cairngorm Reindeer Support Scheme, individuals and organisations can assist in maintaining this unique herd of Reindeer in Scotland, which is dependent upon your support, by taking a financial stake in its upkeep. Reindeer supporters contribute with a support fee of £25.00* (£30.00* outside UK) which provides maintenance for one member of the herd for one year. The subscription may be renewed annually. Membership of the scheme entitles the supporter to adopt one Reindeer from the herd for one year. You will receive on registration a Certificate, Information Pack and a few momentoes from the Reindeer Centre. Supporters are encouraged to make enquiries at any time regarding the well-being of the herd.

Notes : Reindeer are not immortal - they do die eventually. More than one person can adopt the same Reindeer.
* For the purposes of V.A.T., this consists of a £1.00 adoption fee and the remainder as a donation.

Application Form

Please return the completed application form to :
The Cairngorm Reindeer Centre, Glenmore, Aviemore, Inverness-shire.
PH22 1QU, Scotland.

Name of Reindeer to be adopted : ....

Please call The Reindeer Centre on (01479) 861228 to verify the availability of the animal of your choice.

Name of Person or Organisation to be included on the Support Certificate :

....
(PLEASE USE BLOCK LETTERS)

Your Name : ....

Address : ....

Telephone No : .... Post Code : ....

☐ Cheque for £25.00 enclosed, payable to The Reindeer Company Limited.
(Payment by cheque can only be accepted from the UK.)

☐ Visa/Mastercard No : ☐☐☐☐☐☐☐☐☐☐☐☐☐☐☐☐☐☐

Card Start Date : .... Expiry Date : .... Adoption Fee: £25 / £30 *

Cardholder's Name : .... (PLEASE PRINT)

If adoption is a gift, please complete this section.
Recipient's Name : ....

Address : ....

Telephone No : .... Post Code : ....

☐ *Please send adoption materials to me by .... (date) for presentation.*
☐ *Please send adoption materials to the recipient to arrive on or before .... (date).*